CW01025067

THE RIBA **STIRLING PRIZE: 20**

To Kevin McCloud – the man who, more than any other,
has made people think about architecture

TONY CHAPMAN

THE RIBA **STIRLING PRIZE**

FOREWORD BY SIR DAVID CHIPPERFIELD

MERRELL
LONDON · NEW YORK

CONTENTS

THE RIBA **STIRLING PRIZE**

FOREWORD

The giving of prizes is a hazardous enterprise at the best of times, but selecting architecture for prizes is an exceptionally complicated task. Objective comparison is difficult enough in the assessment of art or literature, for example, but a building depends on more than the creative talent of the architect alone. Opportunity, client, site, budget and typology all contribute to the built result. For all their limitations, prizes have the virtue of celebrating not only the winners but also, through them, the entire sport, craft or profession.

The Stirling Prize – named after and in tribute to the great architect James Stirling, and from 1998 to 2016 under the inspired stewardship of Tony Chapman at the RIBA – has been a reliable tool in this process. It has managed to bring the subject of architecture into popular consciousness, giving the public an opportunity to debate and consider the importance of the built environment through the focus of a number of carefully selected projects. The Stirling Prize is an annual reminder to the general public of the ambition and the potential of architecture when it is practised at the highest levels.

In daily life, we may struggle to comprehend the forces at work in the construction of the buildings around us, and also to understand why our buildings and our cities look the way they do. Too often we discuss architecture in an anecdotal manner, frequently betraying excessive prejudice or succumbing to the vagaries of taste and superficial opinion. It is not easy to establish a common language that encourages objective debate and understanding. Furthermore, it is difficult to allay the distrust that is routinely displayed by the general public, fuelled by a cocktail of issues, excuses and simplifications, and, above all, by a disappointment in what is built. This scepticism makes it challenging to disentangle the promises of developers, the frustration of planners and the sometimes complicated narratives of architects themselves.

For these reasons, we should support any attempt to promote discourse and appreciation. The Stirling Prize has made an enormous contribution to this effort, for it forces us all – professionals and non-professionals alike – to put aside our prejudices and to think about architecture and its worth. It has created the conditions within which a jury of appointed individuals is tasked with exposing and describing through its selection of shortlisted projects that which is important to the practice and the societal value of architecture.

We should pay tribute to the jury members over these last twenty years. Reaching a verdict is no easy feat, for the jury also has to straddle the territory of architecture itself, taking account of both its passive and active qualities. In some ways, architecture is nothing more than its physical self; it requires no explanation, and conveys its qualities through its presence, celebrating material, light, volume and composition, an intangible chemistry that reveals itself only through the experience of being in the building. On the other hand, architecture is a societal act, representing the values and intentions not only of the architect but also of the client and the community that constructed and use the building. Architecture does not happen by the will of the architect alone; it does not happen naturally, nor does it happen without considerable intent.

Through the theatre of its process over the past two decades, the Stirling Prize has helped to remind us that there is good in architecture and there are good architects – and that architecture should not be ignored or taken for granted.

SIR DAVID CHIPPERFIELD

INTRODUCTION

WHAT DOES STIRLING MEAN?

The answer to that question depends on whom you ask. At its most literal, 'Stirling' means a twentieth-century British architect who wrote cogently, but not extensively: 'It's not a question of style or appearance,' Stirling once wrote, 'it's how you organize spaces and movement for a place and an activity; it's nothing to do with appearance.' He might have been laying down criteria for the prize we named after him. He was also a man who drew beautifully; his coloured sketches were deemed worthy of hanging in the Museum of Modern Art in New York. And he designed early mouth-watering brick-and-concrete buildings before going down with a bad dose of postmodernism from which he never recovered. That was not the cause of his death, however; that was a tragic medical accident.

So what did Stirling mean to the group of people who, four years after Sir James's untimely death in 1992, gathered in a Marylebone restaurant to discuss setting up the prize in his honour? The RIBA already had a Building of the Year, the President's Choice, which sounded more like a poor claret than an architecture prize. This was to be far more democratic. But the main concern of this group – that's Marco Goldschmied, chair of the Awards Group; his predecessor, Jane Priestman; my predecessor, Chris Palmer; and Hugh Pearman, even then architecture critic of *The Sunday Times* – was public relations: how to convince a pathologically sceptical public that architecture is, or should be or can be, a good thing. All architecture prizes do two things: reward and celebrate. That means they give their winners the warm glow of the approbation of their peers (and, with a bit of luck, some cash). And they also celebrate the win, not only with a knees-up, but also, in getting the media on board, by affording the winners greater public recognition. To both these ends, the name of the new prize was important. All agreed it should be named after an architect, not a sponsor (although a sponsor would be nice, eh, Hugh?). They also agreed that he – even with Jane at the table, no one suggested it should be a female architect, or perhaps at the time no one could name one – that *he* should not be able to win it. So, of the 'big names', that ruled out Norman and Richard, Nick and Michael – oh, and yes, Patty. Terry – definitely not. That meant he should either be foreign (foreigners never designed in the UK and still seldom do) or dead. Wren, Hawksmoor – too dead; Corb, Mies – too foreign for a British prize. Or was it a British prize? Marco, true to his European roots, was sure it should not be, that it should be European, whatever that meant. The group plumped for the boundaries of the EU, the membership of which then stood at a manageable and culturally coherent fifteen nations.

Hugh then suggested, if only to change the subject from sponsorship: 'Why not call it the Stirling Prize?' 'Jim would roll in his grave.' 'Why?' 'He hated the RIBA, thought they didn't give him enough work.' 'We are now.' 'Now it's too late.' 'It's not the RIBA's job to …' 'It's the RIBA's job to promote architecture to people who can't even spell it. And "Stirling" would do that – it sounds right, has the right connotations.' 'Yes, silver.' 'That's with an "i", by the way. It *sounds* precious.' 'OK, that's agreed, then.'

At this point, there was talk of prize money that really would make it worth winning, and Hugh promised to rattle some loose change out of his boss Rupert Murdoch's pockets and came up with £20,000. 'At least he can't win it.' 'Who, Murdoch?' 'Jim!' And then Jim went and had the last laugh and did win it in year two with the help of his partner, Michael Wilford, who, when accepting the prize for the Music School in Stuttgart, waved the cheque, not the trophy (designed by Morag Myerscough, by the way, who elegantly won the twentieth Stirling Prize with Allford Hall Monaghan Morris), declaring, 'This is for Jim.' Payback from the RIBA, at last.

These days, the Stirling judging is planned like a military operation – in fact, rather better than many. Back then, it was a bit more hit-and-miss, a case of 'Who can make it, and when?' Even in year three, one judge preferred to visit only the projects that could be reached by helicopter. In 1996 the RIBA President, Owen Luder, was ill, so Jane Priestman took his place, alongside Hugh Pearman and the sculptor Anthony Caro. This meant that no architect judged the first Stirling (sorry, Stephen). Still, I've always said that architecture is too important to leave entirely to architects.

So what did the winners think of Stirling? Stephen Hodder, its first laureate, modestly said he thought he'd won it too early, that the practice was not yet ready to be up there alongside the shortlisted big boys at Aukett and AMEC (yes, they really were shortlisted in year one, along with the more usual suspects Hopkins and a couple of other

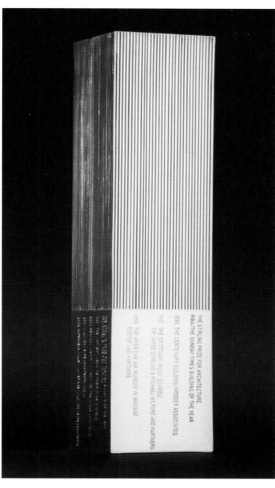

Opposite: James Stirling was best known in the UK for his Tate projects; here, his conversion of the dock buildings in his home city of Liverpool.

Left: The original Stirling Prize trophy. As in the case of the FA Cup, winners' names are inscribed until there is no more space, then a new trophy is commissioned. Both to date have been designed by Morag Myerscough.

A wooden model of Hodder's Centenary Building (winner in 1996), which formed part of the Stirling twentieth-anniversary exhibition at the RIBA in October 2015.

Models of the winning projects made for the Stirling twentieth-anniversary exhibition at the RIBA in October 2015: Alsop & Störmer's Peckham Library, 2000 (top); Wilkinson Eyre's Gateshead Millennium Bridge, 2002 (above); EMBT and RMJM's Scottish Parliament, 2005 (right).

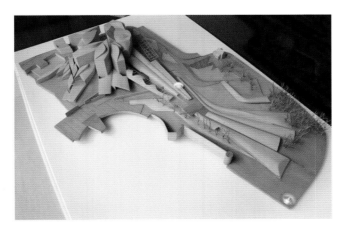

relative unknowns, Morley and Murphy). What was certainly true is that the practice was not set up to pitch for work from the big clients. And awards are a bit like sporting contests: just because you won the FA Cup one year doesn't mean that you're going to win it again the next; you have to start again from scratch. In fact, of the six firms shortlisted in 1996, only one, Hopkins, has got anywhere near to winning the award. Still, Hodder did win the RIBA presidency, and having the Stirling Prize on his CV did him no harm there.

We had to wait until 1999 for the next architects to whom winning Stirling really meant a lot: Future Systems, with the eye-catching Media Centre at Lord's. We were in Glasgow, the first time we'd strayed from the hallowed ground of the RIBA (although we had tried in 1998, but Foster's North Greenwich Transport Interchange for the Dome was not quite ready in time, and we decamped back to the RIBA, where the audience on the tented terrace was kept warm with energetic games of Jenga). Jan Kaplicky again waved the cheque and said, 'This is going straight into the bank on Monday morning.' Thus saving the firm from bankruptcy.

The prize itself still needed a better public platform – something that would get the winner and the shortlisted schemes as much publicity as possible. It didn't require a great leap of imagination for us to come up with the answer. After all, I had been recruited to the world of architecture from the world of television, where I had spent the previous twenty years. In fact, my pitch for the job was that I would get architecture on to TV and into *The Sun*. We did at least manage the first with the help of Stephen Phillips, erstwhile arts correspondent for Channel 4 News. Hence, it was not the BBC that agreed to cover Stirling in 2000, but Channel 4 in the shape of Waldemar Januszczak, who had some militant views on architecture, not all of them flattering. I tried telling an aggrieved RIBA and most of its members that all publicity was good publicity (without believing a word of it). We should have read the runes when, in year one, panicked producers told our live audience that the judges couldn't make up their minds, when in fact they were blamelessly getting drunk in an upper room at the Science Museum, having long since reached their decision. The judges were not half as tipsy, however, as Will Alsop, winner with Peckham Library, who, during his acceptance speech, mysteriously told the planners of Kensington and Chelsea to go forth and multiply. 'Have planners got any better?' I asked him recently. 'No, and neither has architecture. It's got boring. Architects have a duty to provide fun.' And perhaps he is right: architecture has become a whole lot more serious over the twenty years of Stirling; more serious, more rigorous and – perversely perhaps – more popular. When asked at dinner parties what they do, architects no longer have to mumble, 'Something to do with construction.' Now they are the stars of the show.

The real star of the first televised Stirling was not Will or Waldemar, but a man who could not be there, Prime Minister Tony Blair. Marco had written to him with this tempting offer:

I would like to invite you to present this year's Stirling Prize for the Building of the Year. The 2000 RIBA Awards, leading to the Stirling Prize, are to be covered in three programmes on Channel 4, with the presentation to be shown live for the first time. This will give the award the long-overdue status it deserves and place it alongside the Booker and Turner Prizes in the popular imagination. This year we are seeing a number of key projects built with Lottery money opening to the public. Not only are one or two likely to feature on a shortlist for the Stirling Prize, but also they have had the effect of raising the overall standard of RIBA Award winners. Knowing your commitment to design quality and to improving the built environment of this country, I should be grateful if you were able to associate yourself with an award that rewards the architects, clients, engineers and contractors of the best building by a UK architect in the year 2000.

The fact Blair accepted the invitation to present the prize, even if in the end he couldn't make it, shows how much government attitudes to architecture had changed. And he did instead appear by video, saying:

There was a time when people thought that all modern architecture was rubbish and basically the only building that was good was the one you saw in history books. [But design] can make a real difference to the way that people work and live. Good design is not just good for people who work in buildings that are well designed, or live in houses that are well designed; it is also good in terms of crime, safety and the environment. I think there's a whole different type of agenda around architecture and design in public policy terms that would have been considered eccentric five or six years ago.

Kevin McCloud (right) with the first winner of the prize, Stephen Hodder. McCloud presented coverage of the RIBA Stirling Prize on Channel 4 and BBC television nine times between 2003 and 2011.

TV cameraman extraordinaire Tony Etwell, Kevin McCloud's cameraman from the outset.

INTRODUCTION

What is the Stirling effect on the regeneration of our cities? Salford, winner in 1996 (top); Rotherham, winner in 2001 (above); Gateshead, winner in 2002 (opposite, top); Walsall, shortlisted in 2000 (opposite, bottom).

The Waldemar years were a roller coaster; what we needed was someone who was undoubtedly on the side of architecture. I knew Kevin McCloud from the time we'd shared a platform at a Nottingham and Derby Society of Architects event (how far one of us has come) and I'd dissed his producer's mad idea for a programme that would follow the two-year gestation period of the average house-build. Fortunately, they didn't listen to me and they're still making *Grand Designs* some seventeen years later. Kevin loved architecture, and his teasing of architects seemed only to make them and their projects all the more lovable. An ongoing love affair between Kevin and the RIBA ensued, and people watched in their millions. Stirling on TV even survived the poaching of the programme by the BBC – something we could countenance only if it poached Kevin too. Two years later the BBC dropped the broadcast on the ostensible grounds that viewers no longer wanted to watch overpaid architects stuff themselves with dinner. In fact, it came down to money: live TV was becoming too expensive. Of course, the BBC continues to show the winning moments and to make excellent films about the shortlisted schemes, but shows them only on its News Channel.

What of the other winners? Not all were natural TV performers. Will Alsop was, and had the timing and blue language of a stand-up comic. Chris Wilkinson and Jim Eyre, with a win each in 2001 and 2002, were gents, as polite and charming as their architecture. Herzog and de Meuron were absent, but Foster was there in 2004 and shyly gracious. In 2005 Benedetta Tagliabue was genuinely excited. Richard Rogers left it to Ivan Harbour in 2006, but was there in 2009 for an exquisitely painful and funny TV moment, when he was handed the winner's cheque by the man with whom he had very publicly fallen out, his former business partner, Marco Goldschmied, who had stepped up with the prize money when sponsors failed to materialize. In between, David Chipperfield seemed as surprised to win with Marbach in 2007 as the firm was to lose in 2010 with the Neues Museum in Berlin. Zaha Hadid forgave us all for not giving her the prize for BMW or Phaeno when she did the double in 2010 and 2011 with MAXXI and Evelyn Grace. Then came a run of non-favourite winners, the sort of thing that gives the bookies nightmares, but which architects love: Stanton Williams, Witherford Watson Mann, Haworth Tompkins, even Allford Hall Monaghan Morris. They all reacted with characteristic delight and modesty, charming the audience; with Kevin's help, it would have made for great prime-time TV.

What does Stirling mean to the winning places, the towns, cities, even occasionally bits of countryside? Clearly, one successful building can breed success, either because the planners like it and want to encourage more of the same on their patch, or because the client wants to repeat the trick, or other residents or developers want to emulate it. This is called regeneration and it is by no means inevitable, since it depends on many other factors. At its largest scale, it's referred to as the 'Bilbao effect' (in reference to Frank Gehry's Guggenheim Museum in northern Spain), and it requires complicit press, politicians, tourist boards and tourists. It also requires self-belief and the confidence to invest in the unpromising; to overlook the fact that this is Gateshead, not Newcastle; Salford, not Manchester; Rotherham, not Sheffield. There's a pattern here: ugly-sibling syndrome. On three occasions the prize has gone to the less fashionable of a pair of places. What's more, the bigger places have never won the prize. One might wonder why this is. Were the judges deliberately overlooking the greater claims of big-city schemes, or somehow bending over backwards to patronize? I think not; we can and we do judge only as we find. Yet surely architecture generally follows the money. It needs rich or generous clients; that's why 40 per cent of UK architects are based in the southeast of England; that's why London has 'won' the Stirling Prize seven times, with the only other city to have won it more than once being affluent Cambridge, with three wins (and two of them are a stroll apart). I'm sure the prize means a lot to the people of Salford, but one could ask what it has done for the place itself. Salford remains one of the least urbane cities outside North America. Perhaps the 'Bilbao effect' works only if the blockbusters are big enough. They are certainly big in Gateshead: the Millennium Bridge, Sage (a would-be Guggenheim, if ever there was one) and the far more tactful Baltic, an old flour mill transformed into a gallery. But these are strung like pearls along the river. Step inland, and all is much as it was in the 1980s and '90s.

And what of Rotherham/Sheffield? Magna is great and continues to pull in the punters (unlike Sheffield's National Centre for Popular Music), but its hinterland still resembles a post-industrial wasteland linked by urban motorways. Jonathan Meades, suspicious as ever of the easy one-liner,

Top: The Stirling judges in 2007, Alain de Botton (obscured), Kieran Long, Sunand Prasad, Tom Bloxham and Louisa Hutton, are shown around Casa de Música by Ellen van Loon of OMA.

Above: Glenn Howells (centre) shows Alain de Botton (left) and the 2007 jury chair, Sunand Prasad, around the Savill Building.

describes Bilbao as 'the most importunate building of the recent past. It screams deafeningly: take my picture ... but only from my good side. ... If architecture is frozen music, then Gehry has devised a very catchy jingle.' Stirling can be like that, concentrating, if we are not very careful, on the obviously photogenic. Fortunately, visits usually lift the illusory veil. Or else the reality proves even better than the image. The projects are seldom what the pictures would have us believe.

So what does it mean *not* to win the Stirling Prize? In short: as much as it means to win it. Ask five-times-shortlisted O'Donnell + Tuomey, forever the Stirling bridesmaid, although recipient of the Royal Gold Medal. Ask Hopkins, a firm not dissimilar in its care and craft, but one that has tended to fall on its sword, insisting that the superlative Westminster Underground station be judged alongside the unexceptional Portcullis House. In the case of Hopkins's Velodrome, Olympic organizers and security advisers prevented the Stirling judges getting a proper look at the exterior before herding them inside.

Many architects simply cannot believe it when they don't win. For instance, when I went over to commiserate with Zaha about Phaeno not winning, she declared, 'I will never enter your awards again.' And she didn't – not for a year, anyway. Some resort to dark humour to mask their disappointment: 'At least we won the cold-dip galvanizing award', said Nick Grimshaw when Eden lost out to Magna. When the elemental Downland Gridshell was pipped at the post by Gateshead Millennium Bridge, Ted Cullinan pondered, 'How can we compete with that beauty doing its song-and-dance routine outside the judging room?' Sheila O'Donnell and John Tuomey were simply reduced to tears more than once.

Some firms seem to go out of their way not to win the prize. Others perform so well on the visits that they hugely shorten their odds. Of course, it shouldn't matter; the judges are no more there to judge performance than they are to judge a beauty contest. Yet it does matter. Four of those who won against the favourites did so because they made their presentation a team effort. In 2008 Accordia made merit of its three architects and then threw in its architect-planner, Peter Studdert, the man who for many years was effectively Cambridge's city architect. In 2013 Witherford Watson Mann staged a combative and funny double act

Below: Shadow and light play on the faces of the 2009 judges Benedetta Tagliabue, Stirling winner in 2005, and Thomas Heatherwick, designer.

Right: What impressed the Stirling judges about Liverpool One (shortlisted in 2009) was not the showpiece architecture, but the quality of the background stuff.

New guard in 2009: Richard Rogers (left) looks sceptical of recently appointed partner Ivan Harbour's explanation of their Maggie's in Hammersmith. Sir John Sorrell, one of the Stirling judges, listens intently.

In 2009, Richard Rogers is handed the winner's cheque by Marco Goldschmied, former managing director of Richard Rogers Partnership and sponsor of that year's Stirling Prize.

Top: The 2011 Stirling judges – (from left) Peter Cook, Angela Brady, Alison Brooks, Hanif Kara and Dan Pearson – at the Angel Building.

Above: Judges Peter Cook (left) and Hanif Kara cast their eyes over the eventual 2011 winner, Zaha Hadid's Evelyn Grace Academy in Brixton.

with Steve Witherford and client Anna Keay. Judging can be an overly serious business, and some levity can help, especially when the weather is less than cheerful. It poured throughout the visit. Then Haworth Tompkins went one better with a triple act: Steve Tompkins, a man who could well have trodden the boards he designs, bouncing off two sparky clients. And finally AHMM, who cast aside PowerPoint presentations and choreographed a visit to perfection, with clients, artists, landscape architects and engineers popping up in surprisingly appropriate places. It could all have been too much; that it wasn't was due to Paul Monaghan's passion and wit. Anyway, it's far better to over-organize a visit than restage any number of the stumbling tours of yesteryear. Or maybe is it just that, after twenty years, architects are getting better at staging visits. Note that three of those four were in the last three years.

All of which raises the question of whether the Stirling judges go out of their way to do things differently: do they set out to surprise us? Based on my experience of twenty of the prizes, I don't believe they do. I don't think they set out to do anything other than find the best buildings among those presented to them in that year. This may not be the case with other prizes, but the Stirling winner does not depend on some agenda laid down by the organizing committee, nor even by the chair. The Pritzker Prize has a standing jury, and some members have been on their feet a long time. A couple of years ago, the Pritzker committee decided it should be looking at work on the basis of its contribution to society. It became overnight a prize about societal engagement, rather than a kind of lifetime-achievement award. Recent laureates Shigeru Ban and Alejandro Aravena are excellent architects, but both still have with much to do in their careers. One might ask if that matters. Does it matter if the RIBA's Honours Committee, which chooses the Royal Gold Medallist, surprises with its decisions? Probably not. Foster, Rogers and Chipperfield were all in their forties when they won the Gold Medal, and few would gainsay their receipt of the award. The opposite pertains, too: architects can go past their sell-by date. Grimshaw has never won, neither did the Smithsons, who died before they could do so.

Stirling is not like this. Some call it a snapshot, but if that were true, it wouldn't take seventy-odd people to produce the winner, with four stages of judging. I prefer

Top: Dame Zaha Hadid, twice winner of the RIBA Stirling Prize, gives the Royal Gold Medal Lecture less than two months before her untimely death in 2016.

Centre: Kevin McCloud interviews 2010 Stirling judges Ivan Harbour (left) and Edward Jones.

Above: Angela Brady, RIBA President, presents Patrik Schumacher of Zaha Hadid Architects with the 2011 Stirling Prize for the Evelyn Grace Academy.

Top: Stanton Williams won the Stirling Prize in 2012 for the Sainsbury Laboratory. Left to right: Angela Brady, RIBA President; Alan Stanton; Lord Sainsbury, project sponsor; Paul Williams; Gavin Henderson of Stanton Williams; and Roger Freedman, chief scientific adviser.

Centre: David Sillito (second right) of the BBC interviews William Mann and Steve Witherford, winners of

the Stirling Prize in 2013, for Astley Castle, and the client, Anna Keay, in Stanton Williams's Granary Building, King's Cross.

Above: Steve Tompkins gives the acceptance speech for the 2014 Stirling Prize, for the Everyman Theatre, watched by the RIBA President, Stephen Hodder (left); the client, Gemma Bodinetz; and Graham Haworth (right).

INTRODUCTION

Top: A view of the Stirling twentieth-anniversary exhibition held at the RIBA in October 2015.

Above: Previous winners gather at the RIBA prior to the presentation of the 2015 Stirling Prize – which at least explains the absence of Paul Monaghan and Simon Allford.

to think of it as a carefully composed study. And like all art, judging is an editing process: all the elements, all the possibilities are considered. What is left out shapes what remains. The sculptor best exemplifies this process, chipping away at a block of stone until, magically, what remains is a piece of art. High Court judges do much the same thing, weighing up the evidence until they arrive finally at a verdict beyond all reasonable doubt. The judging we do is every bit as rigorous and almost as important.

And what does Stirling mean to clients? The RIBA takes very seriously the essential role that a client plays in the creation of great architecture. It has given clients their own special award for nearly as long as it has presented Stirling. This is no mere lip service; clients do not only pick up the tab, they also help to shape the winning buildings. The prize is presented to the architects *and the clients* of the building that has made the greatest contribution to the evolution of architecture. Maybe that is why the Stirling-winning client seldom wins the Client of the Year, the Media Centre and the MCC being rare 'joint winners'. Some of the wisest words spoken about clients came from Frank Gehry when he was presented with the Royal Gold Medal in 2000: 'Different clients keep you on your toes and keep you from repeating yourself. If I didn't have a client, I'd probably build the same damned thing over and over again. But it's also been important to pick my clients and be careful about it and to work with those I'm comfortable with and who are willing to become partners in the effort.'

Finally, consider the other partners in architecture: the public, the people who buy architecture, not directly as clients but as taxpayers, as members of this or that, or who use it as pupils, patients, shoppers, worshippers, etc. What does Stirling mean to them, and what would they make of these twenty buildings? They would look a bit odd, corralled into an architectural zoo. The Museum of Modern Literature and the Sainsbury Laboratory would probably get on in a polite kind of way, perhaps deigning to talk to the Centenary Building. Peckham Library and the Media Centre would out-jostle each other for attention. There'd be a backyard for the grunge: Magna, maybe Laban for its setting, and the Everyman (although Haworth Tompkins has done grungier). The Music School would be hanging around on the edge of things, with no one much to talk to, wondering whether to join the enclave of some of the other expats – the Scottish

Parliament and MAXXI – in one way or another, or whether to muscle in on the neo-brutalist schools, Burntwood and the Evelyn Grace Academy. There'd be a glass menagerie accommodating the Foster siblings: 30 St Mary Axe and Duxford. And in a cosy corner would be Accordia, Maggie's and Astley – a little surprised to be invited, but pleased to be flying the flag for housing, health care and conservation. After all, nothing is more important than sheltering and healing, or saving and building on the best of our past.

Like all good parties (and Stirling has produced some of the best over the years), much depends on the strength of the guest list, however it's arrived at. This list of winners does not make any definitive statements about the state of architecture in the late twentieth and early twenty-first centuries. Except to say that architecture is in a hell of a better state than it was when Stirling – and I – started off twenty years ago.

Paul Monaghan celebrates with the RIBA Awards Manager, Jennifer Kean, after winning the Stirling Prize in 2015.

Top: The author taking pictures at an exhibition.

Above: The 2015 winning team: AHMM, their clients, consultants and contractors. Paul Monaghan holds the trophy, with its designer, Morag Myerscough, to his left.

1996–2005

1996
WINNER
THE CENTENARY BUILDING, UNIVERSITY OF SALFORD
Salford, Greater Manchester
HODDER ASSOCIATES

1997
WINNER
THE MUSIC SCHOOL
Stuttgart, Germany
MICHAEL WILFORD & PARTNERS

1998
WINNER
AMERICAN AIR MUSEUM IN BRITAIN, IMPERIAL WAR MUSEUM
Duxford, Cambridge
FOSTER + PARTNERS

1999
WINNER
NATWEST MEDIA CENTRE, LORD'S CRICKET GROUND
St John's Wood Road, London NW8
FUTURE SYSTEMS

2000
WINNER
PECKHAM LIBRARY AND MEDIA CENTRE
Peckham Hill Street, London SE15
ALSOP & STÖRMER

2001
WINNER
MAGNA SCIENCE ADVENTURE CENTRE
Rotherham, South Yorkshire
WILKINSON EYRE ARCHITECTS

2002
WINNER
GATESHEAD MILLENNIUM BRIDGE
Gateshead, Tyne and Wear
WILKINSON EYRE ARCHITECTS

2003
WINNER
LABAN
Creekside, London SE8
HERZOG & DE MEURON

2004
WINNER
30 ST MARY AXE
London EC3
FOSTER + PARTNERS

2005
WINNER
THE SCOTTISH PARLIAMENT
Horse Wynd, Edinburgh
EMBT AND RMJM

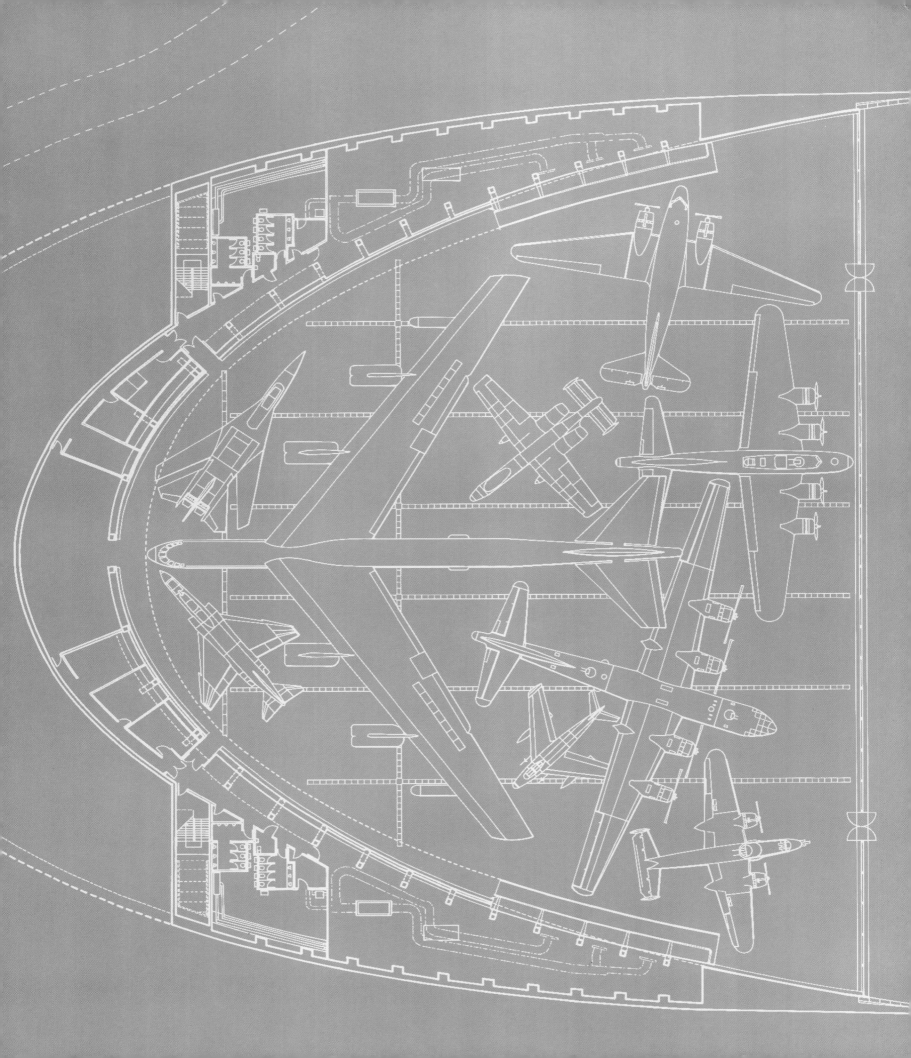

1996

THE CENTENARY BUILDING, UNIVERSITY OF SALFORD

Salford, Greater Manchester

HODDER ASSOCIATES
JOINT WINNER OF THE RIBA ARCHITECTURE IN EDUCATION AWARD

The subtly curved front elevation of
the Centenary Building at dusk.

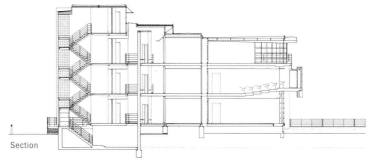

Section

Stephen Hodder's internal street treats students as mature members of the society of which they will soon be part.

When setting the brief, the client described the function of the building as a 'fusion of design and technology', and asked that the building reflect this fusion. The result is a layered building in both plan and section, and it is this layering that gives it its remarkable qualities.

The centre, which is situated on the threshold between the city and the academic campus, houses the departments of Interior Architecture, Design Studies, and Graphic and Industrial Design, with a total of 400 students. The first four-storey layer of the building, an orthogonal strip facing eastwards towards the town, provides simple rectangular studios and seminar rooms. It is separated from the second layer – a three-storey strip of cellular rooms for tutors – by a top-lit internal street. Behind the tutors' room is a third layer, which faces inwards towards the rest of the college, accommodating CAD suites, lecture theatres and studios.

Inside, this building has a very special quality: the tall, narrow internal street is dynamic; top light washes down one side and is complemented by artificial light. Despite being built quickly (the team had to be on site just twelve weeks after appointment) and inexpensively, the centre is a modern and sophisticated exercise in steel, glass and concrete. Materials, architectural detailing and colouring – grey, silver and white – are cool. The architects have bowed out the main façade to create a wide studio and lecture-theatre space with indirect daylighting, breaking the internal street with asymmetrical galleries and bridges, and exposing rooms to this central space to impart an air of purpose and animation. These qualities are reinforced by the architects' decision to deny some rooms windows, giving them instead fully-glazed internal walls.

This is a building that responds in a symbolic and particular way to its brief and setting, but at the same time succeeds in creating a whole that is cool and crisp, dynamic and complex – a distinguished achievement indeed.

Commenting on the first Stirling shortlist [overleaf], the RIBA President, Owen Luder, said: 'The standard of entries demonstrates a high level of innovation and imagination across a range of building types, in particular in higher education. It is also fascinating to see in the names of Morley, Hodder and Murphy the rise of a new and younger generation of architects. But Hodder's building is by far the most complex and ambitious, and a worthy winner of the first Stirling Prize.'

CLIENT
University of Salford

STRUCTURAL ENGINEER
Stephen Morley Partnership

CONTRACTOR
AMEC Design and Management

CONTRACT VALUE
£3.6 million

IMAGES
Dennis Gilbert – VIEW

1996

D10 BUILDING, THE BOOTS COMPANY
Thane Road, Nottingham

AMEC DESIGN AND MANAGEMENT
WINNER OF THE RIBA DULUX HERITAGE COLOURS
CONSERVATION AWARD

CLIENT
The Boots Company

STRUCTURAL ENGINEER/CONTRACTOR
AMEC Design and Management

CONTRACT VALUE
£20 million

**MCC INDOOR CRICKET SCHOOL,
LORD'S CRICKET GROUND**
St John's Wood Road, London NW8

DAVID MORLEY ARCHITECTS
WINNER OF THE RIBA ARCHITECTURE IN SPORT
AND LEISURE AWARD

CLIENT
Marylebone Cricket Club

STRUCTURAL ENGINEER
Price & Myers

CONTRACTOR
Wates Construction (London)

CONTRACT VALUE
£2 million

PROCTER & GAMBLE HEADQUARTERS
Weybridge, Surrey

AUKETT ASSOCIATES
WINNER OF THE RIBA COMMERCIAL ARCHITECTURE
AWARD

CLIENT
Procter & Gamble – Health and Beautycare

STRUCTURAL ENGINEERS
Aukett Associates; Anthony Hunt Associates

CONTRACTOR
Costain Construction

CONTRACT VALUE
£20 million

SHORTLISTED

THE QUEEN'S BUILDING, EMMANUEL COLLEGE, UNIVERSITY OF CAMBRIDGE
St Andrew's Street, Cambridge

MICHAEL HOPKINS AND PARTNERS
JOINT WINNER OF THE RIBA ARCHITECTURE
IN EDUCATION AWARD

CLIENT
Emmanuel College, University of Cambridge

STRUCTURAL ENGINEER
Buro Happold

CONTRACTOR
Sir Robert McAlpine

CONTRACT VALUE
£4.3 million

SHORTLISTED

17 ROYAL TERRACE MEWS
Edinburgh

RICHARD MURPHY ARCHITECTS
WINNER OF THE RIBA IBSTOCK AWARD FOR HOUSES
AND HOUSING

CLIENT
Carol Høgel

STRUCTURAL ENGINEER
David Narro Associates

CONTRACTOR
Inscape Joinery

CONTRACT VALUE
£190,000

JUDGES

OWEN LUDER
RIBA President (chair)

SIR ANTHONY CARO
Sculptor

HUGH PEARMAN
Architecture critic of
The Sunday Times

JANE PRIESTMAN
Chair of the RIBA Awards Group

1997

THE MUSIC SCHOOL
Stuttgart, Germany

MICHAEL WILFORD & PARTNERS
JOINT WINNER OF THE RIBA ARCHITECTURE IN EDUCATION AWARD

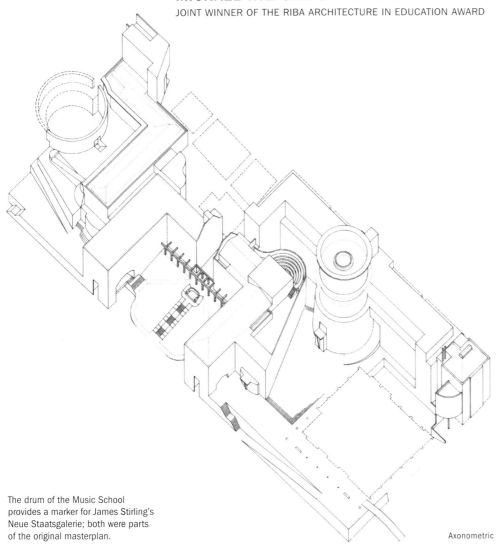

The drum of the Music School provides a marker for James Stirling's Neue Staatsgalerie; both were parts of the original masterplan.

Axonometric

The Music School, together with the History Museum (then under construction), completes the sequence of public buildings in the urban masterplan conceived for Stuttgart's 'Cultural Mile' flanking Konrad-Adenauer Strasse, and continues the series of external semi-enclosed spaces opening towards the city, initiated by the adjacent Neue Staatsgalerie. A new raised plaza, framed by the Music School, History Museum and existing Landtag building, is the focus of the composition.

The school has nine floors with accommodation for students and public. The chamber music/lecture hall, the 450-seat concert hall and the library are located in a tower on the plaza, registering the presence of the Music School on the city's skyline. Entrance to the school is via a four-storey foyer that provides multiple connections and serves as the main public vestibule. There is also accommodation for the departments of Music Theory, Composition and Pitch, as well as practice and teaching rooms, and a senate room with its own rooftop terrace for receptions or small concerts.

The building is a classically inspired work of great power and subtlety that can be directly compared to the work of the interwar Scandinavian master Gunnar Asplund. The battered and perforated cylinder of the tower is set against, and cut into, the rectilinear block of the main building, so setting up a tension that is resolved with exceptional clarity within, right down to the arrangement of the pipes in the great organ in the flamboyantly colourful concert hall. Above the hall is the library, with its double-height perimeter and giant-scale bookshelves. This is a building that surprises, inspires and demands to be visited.

The Music School at Stuttgart was the last building that Sir James Stirling worked on before his death in 1992. The designs were completed by Michael Wilford and other members of the partnership. The school is unusual in being a late example of the neglected British monumental tradition. This architectural strand ran in the twentieth century from Edwin Lutyens through Basil Spence to Denys Lasdun and Stirling, and from Stirling to his long-term professional partner, Wilford. Massive, beautifully made and ingeniously sited, the Music School is – and this was one lesson of the Stirling judges' European venture – of a quality that is rare indeed, not just in the British college system, but anywhere at all in the United Kingdom.

Below: The rich colours of the interiors, in particular of the organ in the concert hall, represent one of the last hurrahs of European postmodernism.

Below, right: The keep-like design of the tower (complete with holes that might be used as arrow slits to ward off attackers) is appropriate to its position overlooking the city.

CLIENT
Land Baden-Württemberg

STRUCTURAL ENGINEERS
Ove Arup & Partners; Boll und Partner

CONTRACTOR
Wolff & Müller

CONTRACT VALUE
DM90 million

IMAGES
Richard Bryant – Arcaid

1997

SHORTLISTED

LE GRAND BLEU (REGIONAL GOVERNMENT HEADQUARTERS)
Marseilles, France

ALSOP & STÖRMER
WINNER OF THE RIBA CIVIC AND COMMUNITY ARCHITECTURE AWARD

CLIENT
Conseil Général des Bouches-du-Rhône

STRUCTURAL ENGINEER
Ove Arup & Partners

CONTRACT VALUE
FF883.5 million

SHORTLISTED

LONDON UNDERGROUND STRATFORD MARKET DEPOT
Burford Road, London E15

CHRIS WILKINSON ARCHITECTS
WINNER OF THE RIBA COMMERCIAL ARCHITECTURE AWARD

CLIENT
LUL Jubilee Line Extension Project Team

STRUCTURAL ENGINEER
Hyder Consulting

MAIN CONTRACTOR
John Laing Construction

CONTRACT VALUE
£18 million

SHORTLISTED

MAGGIE KESWICK JENCKS CANCER CARING CENTRE, WESTERN GENERAL HOSPITAL
Crewe Road, Edinburgh

RICHARD MURPHY ARCHITECTS
WINNER OF THE RIBA ARCHITECTURE IN HEALTHCARE AWARD

CLIENT
Maggie's

STRUCTURAL ENGINEER
David Narro Associates

MAIN CONTRACTOR
Peter Moran

CONTRACT VALUE
£127,900

SHORTLISTED

PAUL HAMLYN LEARNING RESOURCE CENTRE, THAMES VALLEY UNIVERSITY

Slough, Berkshire

RICHARD ROGERS PARTNERSHIP

JOINT WINNER OF THE RIBA ARCHITECTURE IN EDUCATION AWARD

CLIENT
Thames Valley University

STRUCTURAL ENGINEER
Buro Happold

MAIN CONTRACTOR
John Laing Construction

CONTRACT VALUE
£3.6 million

SHORTLISTED

ROOFTOP APARTMENT

Paris, France

MARK GUARD ARCHITECTS

WINNER OF THE RIBA HOUSES AND HOUSING AWARD

CLIENT
Chris Avery

STRUCTURAL ENGINEER
Michael Baigent Orla Kelly

MAIN CONTRACTOR
Metrotech & Co.

CONTRACT VALUE
£118,440

JUDGES

DAVID ROCK
RIBA President (chair)

MARCO GOLDSCHMIED
Director of Richard Rogers Partnership and Chair of the RIBA Awards Group

STEPHEN HODDER
Architect and Stirling Prize winner in 1996

HUGH PEARMAN
Architecture critic of *The Sunday Times*

CHARLES SAUMAREZ SMITH
Director of the National Portrait Gallery

1998

WINNER

AMERICAN AIR MUSEUM IN BRITAIN, IMPERIAL WAR MUSEUM
Duxford, Cambridge

FOSTER + PARTNERS
JOINT WINNER OF THE RIBA SPORT AND LEISURE AWARD

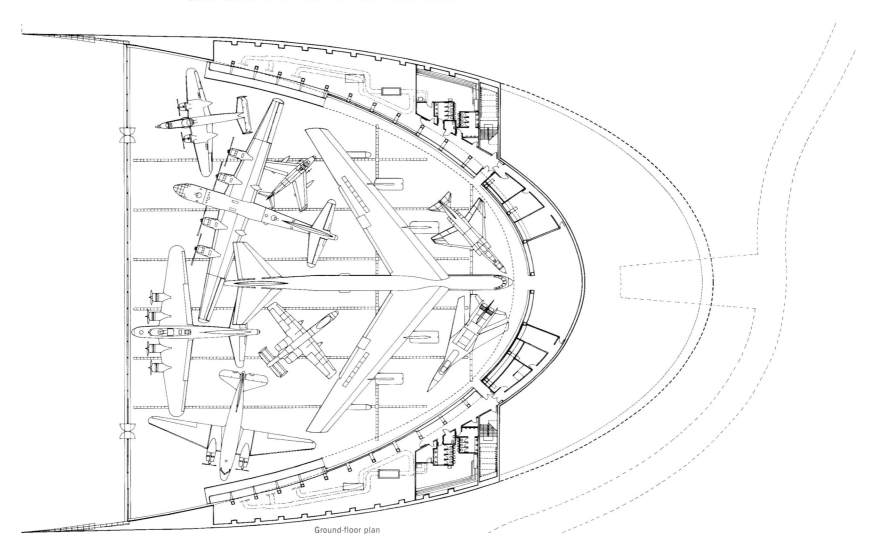

Ground-floor plan

CLIENT
Imperial War Museum

STRUCTURAL ENGINEER
Ove Arup & Partners

CONTRACTOR
John Sisk & Son

CONTRACT VALUE
£7.95 million

IMAGES
Nigel Young – Foster + Partners

In 1986 the Imperial War Museum asked Foster + Partners to design a museum to house its collection of American aircraft of the Second World War that had flown from East Anglian bases, including Duxford, a Royal Air Force and US Army Air Forces fighter station during that conflict. One such aircraft is a B-52 Stratofortress bomber so large that its shape determined the form of the building. The dramatically curved roof is partially dug into the landscape, and the abrupt slice of the building's façade, measuring 90 metres by 18.5 metres, gives sweeping views on to the runway. This glass wall is fully demountable, allowing aircraft to be rolled into and out of the museum. Visitors approach through a tunnel-like entrance and find themselves facing the nose of the bomber. The 16-metre tail fin and its 61-metre wingspan mean the aircraft all but touches the

roof and sides of the building. Other aircraft stand around it or are hung from suspension points in the ceiling. Even though they weigh up to 10 tonnes each, they look like toys against the mass of the B-52, so symbolic of the Cold War.

The double-skinned roof, which uses precast concrete panels, was developed in collaboration with Ove Arup. Its single span is the largest of its kind in Europe, its apparent simplicity belying the effort involved. The stresses created by aircraft being hung from the roof mean that a thick shell is required, one that is also double-curved – that is, in which the radii change constantly in two directions. Arup has created just six concrete components to achieve this.

The success of the project lies in the resonance between the elegant engineered form of the building and the technically driven shapes of the aeroplanes that it contains.

36

Below: Foster's window on the airfield can be removed when exhibits need to be moved or maintained.

Bottom: The curved walkways give visitors the impression of being suspended in the air, much like the aircraft on display.

The building itself sustains the fascination of these objects, reassembling them and presenting them back to the visitor with dramatic intensity. Taking its inspiration from a range of building forms associated with war, from the humble Anderson shelter to hard high-explosive-proof aircraft hangars, the museum rises smoothly out of the ground to make a big window on to the airfield.

The project has a quality beyond that of simply being a museum; it is a memorial to the USAAF in the Second World War. The concrete roof structure conveys a feeling of compression that emphasizes the power of a simple idea. This is definitely a 'less is more' building.

1998

SHORTLISTED

THE BRITISH LIBRARY
Euston Road, London NW1

COLIN ST JOHN WILSON
& PARTNERS

CLIENT
The Board of the British Library

STRUCTURAL ENGINEER
Ove Arup & Partners

CONTRACTORS
Laing Management (Phase 1a);
McAlpine Haden Joint Venture (completion)

CONTRACT VALUE
£511 million

Although the project was overlooked for an RIBA Civic and Community Architecture Award, the judges agreed to consider it for the Stirling Prize in view of the immensity of its achievement.

SHORTLISTED

COMMERZBANK HEADQUARTERS
Frankfurt am Main, Germany

FOSTER + PARTNERS
JOINT WINNER OF THE RIBA COMMERCIAL
ARCHITECTURE AWARD

CLIENT
Immobilienvermietungsgesellschaften
Alpha + Beta

STRUCTURAL ENGINEERS
Ove Arup & Partners with Krebs + Kiefer

CONTRACTOR
Hochtief

CONTRACT VALUE
DM525 million

SHORTLISTED

CRYSTAL PALACE CONCERT PLATFORM
Crystal Palace Park, London SE26

IAN RITCHIE ARCHITECTS
JOINT WINNER OF THE RIBA SPORT AND
LEISURE AWARD

CLIENT
London Borough of Bromley

STRUCTURAL ENGINEER
Atelier One

CONTRACTOR
Ballast Wiltshier

CONTRACT VALUE
£830,000

SHORTLISTED

QUAY BAR
Deansgate Quay, Manchester

STEPHENSON BELL ARCHITECTS
JOINT WINNER OF THE RIBA SPORT AND
LEISURE AWARD

CLIENT
Wolverhampton and Dudley Breweries

STRUCTURAL ENGINEER
Peter Taylor Associates

CONTRACTOR
Roland Bardsley

CONTRACT VALUE
£1.25 million

SHORTLISTED

RICHARD ATTENBOROUGH CENTRE FOR DISABILITY AND THE ARTS, UNIVERSITY OF LEICESTER
Lancaster Road, Leicester

IAN TAYLOR WITH BENNETTS ASSOCIATES
WINNER OF THE RIBA EDUCATION AND HEALTH AWARD
(SPONSORED BY THE DEPARTMENT OF HEALTH)

CLIENT
Simon Britton, Director of Estates, University of Leicester

STRUCTURAL ENGINEER
Curtins Consulting Engineers

CONTRACTOR
John Laing Construction

CONTRACT VALUE
£1.15 million

SHORTLISTED

ST BENNO-GYMNASIUM
Dresden, Germany

BEHNISCH, BEHNISCH
& PARTNER
WINNER OF THE RIBA ARCHITECTURE IN EDUCATION
AWARD

CLIENT
Bistum Dresden-Meissen

STRUCTURAL ENGINEER
Fritz Wenzel

CONSTRUCTION MANAGEMENT
BB&P

CONTRACT VALUE
DM49.5 million

KAISTRASSE OFFICE BUILDING
Düsseldorf, Germany

**DAVID CHIPPERFIELD ARCHITECTS
WITH INGENHOVEN OVERDIEK
KAHLEN UND PARTNER**
JOINT WINNER OF THE RIBA COMMERCIAL
ARCHITECTURE AWARD

CLIENT
GbR Kaistrasse

STRUCTURAL ENGINEER
Arup GmbH

CONTRACTOR
Strabag Bau

CONTRACT VALUE
£3 million

SHORTLISTED

**LANDESGIROKASSE BANK CENTRAL
ADMINISTRATION BUILDING**
Stuttgart, Germany

BEHNISCH, BEHNISCH & PARTNER
JOINT WINNER OF THE RIBA COMMERCIAL
ARCHITECTURE AWARD

CLIENT
Landesgirokasse

STRUCTURAL ENGINEER
Leonhardt, Andrä und Partner

CONSTRUCTION MANAGEMENT
BB&P with Hans-Joachim Maile

CONTRACT VALUE
DM2 million

SHORTLISTED

PRIVATE HOUSE IN HAMPSTEAD
London NW3

RICK MATHER ARCHITECTS
WINNER OF THE RIBA HOUSES AND HOUSING AWARD

CLIENT
Private

STRUCTURAL ENGINEER
Atelier One

CONTRACTOR
Hosier & Dickinson

CONTRACT VALUE
£750,000

SHORTLISTED

**TEMPLE OF CONCORD AND VICTORY, STOWE
LANDSCAPE GARDENS**
Buckingham, Buckinghamshire

**PETER INSKIP + PETER JENKINS
ARCHITECTS**
WINNER OF THE RIBA CONSERVATION AWARD

CLIENT
National Trust for Places of Historic Interest or Natural Beauty

STRUCTURAL ENGINEER
Ralph Mills Associates

CONTRACTOR
Linford-Bridgeman

CONTRACT VALUE
£1.5 million

JUDGES

DAVID ROCK
RIBA President (chair)

JAMES DYSON
Designer and industrialist

MARCO GOLDSCHMIED
Chair of the RIBA Awards Group

HUGH PEARMAN
Architecture critic of *The Sunday Times*

MICHAEL WILFORD
Architect and Stirling Prize winner in 1997

1999

NATWEST MEDIA CENTRE, LORD'S CRICKET GROUND
St John's Wood Road, London NW8

FUTURE SYSTEMS
JOINT WINNER OF THE RIBA ARTS AND LEISURE AWARD

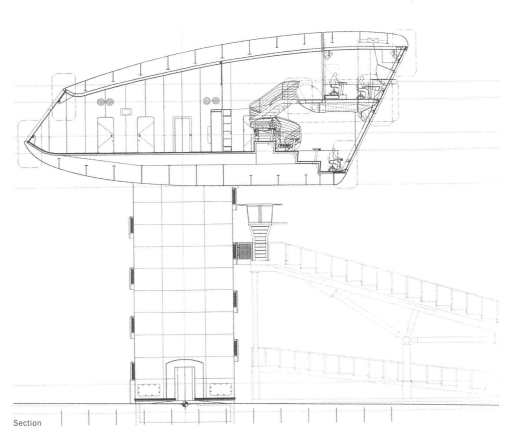

Section

Digital alarm clock, bar-code reader, alien spaceship: these are a few of the attempts by the press to convey an impression of a structure that may at first indeed have seemed alien to its very conventional setting.

This is one instance in which reality has caught up with fiction. An Archigram Walking City pod has marched into Lord's – or rather been borne there on the back of a lorry – and taken up residence. The Media Centre has well and truly been accepted as part of the English summer scene. Future Systems recognized the 'eternal and sacred' atmosphere of the ground in its competition entry, yet came up with a structure that is entirely new. The structure's soft lines, not least in its less-photographed back, reflect not only its origins in a Cornish boatyard, but also mirror the sweeping curves of the stands. The interior is as comfortable and luxurious as a 1950s Chevrolet, the baby-blue upholstery of which inspired it.

The NatWest Media Centre became an instant icon; a large white eye on the world of cricket, communicating the MCC's belief in the future of the game, and contrasting almost irreverently with the traditional pavilion it faces. The simple design clearly communicates its purpose and imposes itself on this historic arena, thus avoiding the risk of becoming just another charm on the Lord's bracelet. The structure suggests a new world of off-site manufacturing and a level of consistent quality that (sadly) is more associated with the car industry than with the business of construction. One of the most impressive aspects of the design is the way in which it neatly avoids the age-old problems of scale, mass and context, which traditional forms find difficult to transcend. These issues just do not apply to its sleek form.

Today the Media Centre is a TV personality. It is its own thing, completely unusual and totally uncompromising. It is a breath of architectural fresh air. Talking to lay judge Stella McCartney, the Stirling jury chair, Marco Goldschmied, sat himself in the press box and declared, 'This is the best seat in the house, forget the Long Room.'

This project is a complete one-off: a wacky solution to a singular problem. Future Systems had been wanting to do this for a long time, and there is something brilliant about having a dream and seeing it through. This was at last the twentieth century – in the nick of time. It may or may not be the future, but it certainly works.

CLIENT
Marylebone Cricket Club

STRUCTURAL ENGINEER
Ove Arup & Partners

CONTRACTOR
Pendennis Shipyard

CONTRACT VALUE
£5 million

IMAGES
Richard Davies

Opposite: Journalists in the Media Centre feel as cosseted as the members in the pavilion opposite.

Above and right: With the ground full for a Test match or empty, the Media Centre represents a new image for English cricket.

1999

THE MUSEUM OF SCOTLAND
Chambers Street, Edinburgh

BENSON + FORSYTH
STIRLING PRIZE RUNNER-UP

CLIENT
Trustees of the National Museums of Scotland

STRUCTURAL ENGINEER
Anthony Hunt Associates

CONTRACTOR
Bovis Construction (Scotland)

CONTRACT VALUE
£44.85 million

SHORTLISTED

NORTH GREENWICH UNDERGROUND STATION
Millennium Way, London SE10

**ALSOP LYALL & STÖRMER
WITH JLE PROJECT TEAM**
JOINT WINNER OF THE RIBA CIVIC AND COMMUNITY
ARCHITECTURE AWARD

CLIENT
London Underground

STRUCTURAL ENGINEER
Benaim Works Joint Venture

CONTRACTORS
Sir Robert McAlpine; Wayss & Freytag

CONTRACT VALUE
£110 million

SHORTLISTED

RANELAGH MULTIDENOMINATIONAL SCHOOL
Dublin, Ireland

O'DONNELL + TUOMEY
WINNER OF THE RIBA EDUCATION AWARD

CLIENT
Ranelagh Multidenominational School

STRUCTURAL ENGINEER
Fearon O'Neill Rooney

CONTRACTOR
Pierce Healy Developments

CONTRACT VALUE
IR£1.16 million

SHORTLISTED

STRATFORD REGIONAL STATION
Station Street, London E15

CHRIS WILKINSON ARCHITECTS
JOINT WINNER OF THE RIBA CIVIC AND COMMUNITY
ARCHITECTURE AWARD

CLIENT
London Underground

STRUCTURAL ENGINEER
Hyder Consulting

CONTRACTOR
Kvaerner Construction

CONTRACT VALUE
£17 million

SHORTLISTED

REICHSTAG, THE NEW GERMAN PARLIAMENT
Berlin, Germany

FOSTER + PARTNERS
WINNER OF THE RIBA CONSERVATION AWARD

CLIENT
Bundesbaugesellschaft Berlin

STRUCTURAL ENGINEERS
Ove Arup & Partners; Schlaich Bergermann Partner; Leonhardt, Andrä und Partner

CONTRACTOR
Büro am Lützowplatz

CONTRACT VALUE
£265 million

SHORTLISTED

THE RIVER & ROWING MUSEUM
Henley-on-Thames, Oxfordshire

DAVID CHIPPERFIELD ARCHITECTS
JOINT WINNER OF THE RIBA ARTS AND LEISURE AWARD

CLIENT
The River & Rowing Museum Foundation

STRUCTURAL ENGINEER
Whitbybird

CONTRACTOR
Norwest Holst Construction

CONTRACT VALUE
£6 million

SHORTLISTED

STO MARKETING AND TRAINING BUILDING
Stühlingen, Germany

MICHAEL WILFORD & PARTNERS
WINNER OF THE RIBA COMMERCIAL AWARD

CLIENT
Sto

STRUCTURAL ENGINEER
Boll und Partner

CONTRACTOR
Züblin

CONTRACT VALUE
DM15 million

JUDGES

MARCO GOLDSCHMIED
RIBA President (chair)

AMANDA BAILLIEU
Editor of the *RIBA Journal*

STELLA McCARTNEY
Fashion designer

MICHAEL MANSER
Chair of the RIBA Awards Group

RICK MATHER
Architect and Stirling Prize shortlisted in 1998

2000

PECKHAM LIBRARY AND MEDIA CENTRE
Peckham Hill Street, London SE15

ALSOP & STÖRMER

CLIENT
Southwark Education & Leisure Services

STRUCTURAL ENGINEER
Adams Kara Taylor

CONTRACTOR
Sunley Turriff Construction

CONTRACT VALUE
£4.5 million

IMAGES
Gerhard Bissell (opposite); Roderick Coyne (right); Janet Hall (below)

The library, part of the regeneration of Peckham, takes the form of a horizontal block supported on one vertical block and a series of raking angled columns. Further drama is provided by the 2-metre-high stainless-steel letters announcing the building's function, an orange sunshield that looks like a beret, and three internal pods that burst through the roof and add yet further interest to the profile of the library.

The library is Alsop & Störmer's imaginative response to the original brief, which was to 'create a building of architectural merit that will bring prestige to the borough and a welcome psychological boost to the area. It should be a thoroughly modern building that is ahead of its time but also one that does not alienate people by giving an appearance of elitism, strangeness or exclusivity. Local people must be able to relate to the architecture and design as well as the services provided, and they should feel pride in, affection for and ownership of the building.'

One could be excused for suspecting that the unusual, almost folly-like quality of this building would mean that response to function was not at the top of the architects' list of priorities. Nothing could be further from the truth: the library has a new, useful covered square at the entrance; it works internally in a very legible way; and the spaces are one delight after another, with drama never far away.

Peckham Library is popular without being populist. Will Alsop has been known to stick his tongue out at the planners, but here the gesture is friendly; Peckham's planners were on-side from the start.

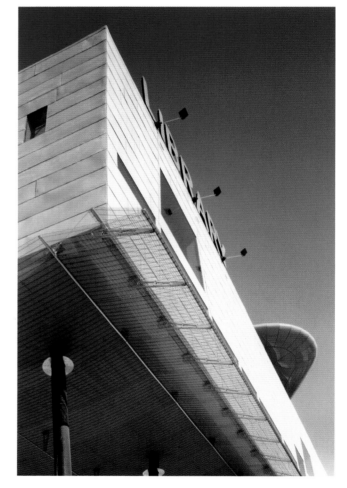

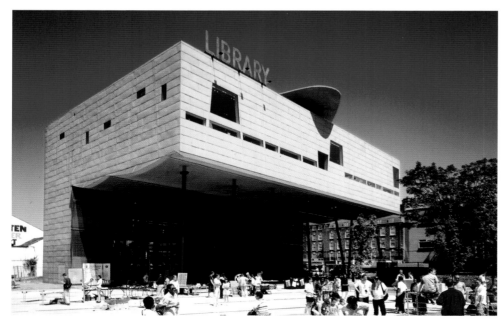

The library is situated in a tough neighbourhood, but the architects have made a virtue of the fact, creating a security grille over the façade that is a thing of delicate beauty in itself, not least in the way it wraps around the underside of the canopy. To produce such an innovative and exciting piece of architecture against the uninspired and uninspiring backdrop of its immediate environs is a real achievement. To have done so on such a relatively low budget is even more remarkable.

The building is full of bravado, and as such it has captured the hearts of a disaffected part of the population. All the best buildings are popular with their users, and the young people of Peckham flock into their library every day. In the end, this is a building to make you smile: more architecture should do that.

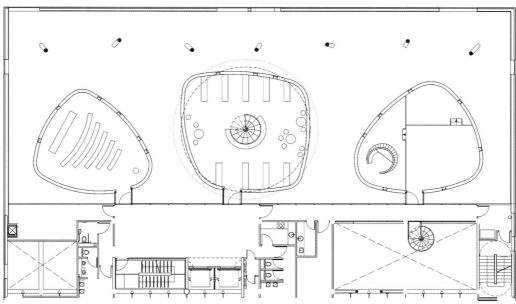

Fifth-floor plan

The timber-clad pods animate the generous space and provide discrete meeting rooms or play spaces.

2000

THE BRITISH AIRWAYS LONDON EYE
Westminster Bridge Road, London SE1

MARKS BARFIELD ARCHITECTS

CLIENT
British Airways London Eye Company

STRUCTURAL ENGINEERS
Babtie Allott & Lomax; Hollandia; Infragroep; Ove Arup & Partners

CONTRACTOR
Mace

CONTRACT VALUE
Confidential

CANARY WHARF UNDERGROUND STATION
Heron Keys Road, London E14

FOSTER + PARTNERS

CLIENT
London Underground

STRUCTURAL ENGINEER
Ove Arup & Partners

CONTRACTOR
Tarmac Bachy Joint Venture

CONTRACT VALUE
£32.5 million

GSW HEADQUARTERS
Berlin, Germany

SAUERBRUCH HUTTON ARCHITECTS

CLIENT
Gemeinnützige Siedlungs- und Wohnungsbaugesellschaft (GSW)

STRUCTURAL/SERVICES ENGINEERS
Arup GmbH; ARGE Arup with IgH

CONTRACTORS
Züblin; Bilfinger Berger

CONTRACT VALUE
£58 million

SHORTLISTED

NEW ART GALLERY WALSALL
Walsall, West Midlands

CARUSO ST JOHN ARCHITECTS

CLIENT
Walsall Metropolitan Borough Council

STRUCTURAL ENGINEER
Ove Arup & Partners

CONTRACTOR
Sir Robert McAlpine

CONTRACT VALUE
£21 million

SHORTLISTED

SAINSBURY'S SUPERMARKET
Bugsby's Way, London SE10

CHETWOOD ASSOCIATES
WINNER OF THE CHANNEL 4 PEOPLE'S CHOICE AWARD

CLIENT
Sainsbury's Supermarkets

STRUCTURAL ENGINEER
WSP Consulting Engineers

SERVICES ENGINEERS
Max Fordham; Oscar Faber

CONTRACTOR
RGCM

CONTRACT VALUE
£13 million

SHORTLISTED

88 WOOD STREET
London EC2

RICHARD ROGERS PARTNERSHIP

CLIENT
Daiwa Europe

STRUCTURAL ENGINEER
Ove Arup & Partners

CONTRACTOR
Kajima UK Engineering

CONTRACT VALUE
£55 million

JUDGES

MICHAEL MANSER
Former RIBA President and Chair of the RIBA
Awards Group (chair)

AMANDA BAILLIEU
Editor of the *RIBA Journal*

TRACEY EMIN
Artist

AMANDA LEVETE
Architect and Stirling Prize winner in 1999

ERIC PARRY
Architect

2001

MAGNA SCIENCE ADVENTURE CENTRE
Rotherham, South Yorkshire

WILKINSON EYRE ARCHITECTS

CLIENT
The Magna Trust

STRUCTURAL ENGINEER
Mott MacDonald

SERVICES ENGINEER
Buro Happold

EXHIBITION DESIGN
Event Communications

LIGHTING DESIGN
Speirs + Major

CONTRACTOR
Schal

CONTRACT VALUE
£37.2 million

IMAGES
Tony Chapman (opposite, top);
Benedict Luxmoore (right; opposite,
bottom)

The Air Pavilion, one of Magna's four
zones dedicated to the elements,
which provide safe, controlled
environments for children amid
the largely untouched spaces
of the steel mill.

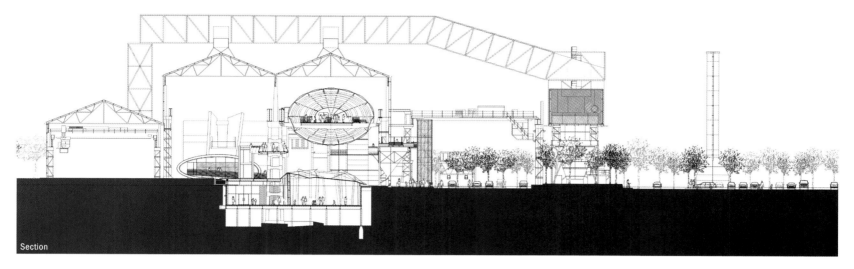
Section

The conversion of the former steelworks was a major Millennium project, additionally funded by English Partnerships and the European Regional Development Fund. Two 350-metre-long bays make up this cathedral-like shed – the biggest building in Britain at the time of its construction during the First World War – but it is the interior that is truly awe-inspiring. The design retains and enhances the excitement of the space, and puts it to use to house exhibitions relating to the four elements of the steel-making process: earth, air, fire and water. The areas are linked by walkways and bridges. Artefacts from the building's past are conserved as evocative sculptures, while video walls recall the human story of steel-making.

Rarely do architects get to work on a project of such vast scale as an abandoned steelworks. Here, the architects have responded with suitably gigantic gestures, but also with an attention to detail in the exhibition areas that combines a necessary robustness with invention and surprise. The integration of architecture, interactive exhibits and highly effective lighting and sound design is relatively seamless, so that visitors oscillate between the compact educational

experiences of the fire, earth, water and air pavilions and revealed fragments of the vastness of the old steelworks. This process is exhilarating, and evokes a sense of awe and excitement in all who visit. Photographs cannot convey the feeling of being inside. The drama of being a small person within a vast black space that is relieved only by gashes of red light, sheets of flame and spots of white light has to be experienced.

Wilkinson Eyre's great achievement, supported by inspired exhibition and lighting design, has been to allow the existing building to speak for itself and tell its own history. The simple device of inserting a walkway that runs centrally through space along the length of the building keeps visitors away from the dirty tackiness of an industrial building only recently abandoned, and allows them to savour its vastness and equally to find their way easily to the exhibits, with the sense of being on a conducted tour. These more orchestrated experiences are handled with panache, but architecturally they are subordinate to the experience of the whole. The result has the obvious rightness that can be achieved only by an inspired and experienced team working with a single-minded client who supported them.

Wilkinson Eyre has applied the same design logic to the exterior, resisting the temptation to spruce up, and allowing the industrial drama to speak for itself.

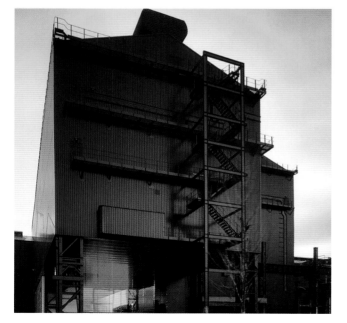

2001

SHORTLISTED

BRITISH EMBASSY

Berlin, Germany

MICHAEL WILFORD & PARTNERS

CLIENT
Overseas Estate Department, Foreign & Commonwealth Office

STRUCTURAL/SERVICES ENGINEERS
Whitbybird with Boll und Partner; Jaeger, Mornhinweg + Partner

CONTRACTOR
Bilfinger Berger

CONTRACT VALUE
PFI project – final figure unknown

SHORTLISTED

EDEN PROJECT

St Austell, Cornwall

NICHOLAS GRIMSHAW & PARTNERS

CLIENT
The Eden Project

STRUCTURAL ENGINEER
Anthony Hunt Associates

SERVICES ENGINEER
Arup

CONTRACTORS
Sir Robert McAlpine; Alfred McAlpine Construction

CONTRACT VALUE
£57 million

SHORTLISTED

THE LAWNS

London N6

ELDRIDGE SMERIN

CLIENTS
Frances and John Sorrell

STRUCTURAL ENGINEER
Arup

CONTRACTOR
Bradford Watts

CONTRACT VALUE
£1.1 million

SHORTLISTED

NATIONAL PORTRAIT GALLERY EXTENSION
St Martin's Place, London WC2

JEREMY DIXON.EDWARD JONES

CLIENT
National Portrait Gallery

STRUCTURAL/SERVICES ENGINEER
Arup

PROJECT MANAGER
Bovis Programme Management

CONTRACTOR
Norwest Holst Construction

CONTRACT VALUE
£13.2 million

SHORTLISTED

PORTCULLIS HOUSE AND WESTMINSTER UNDERGROUND STATION
Bridge Street, London SW1

MICHAEL HOPKINS AND PARTNERS

CLIENTS
Parliamentary Works Directorate; London Underground

STRUCTURAL/CIVIL ENGINEERS
Arup; G. Maunsell & Partners

CONTRACTORS
Laing Management; Balfour Beatty AMEC

CONTRACT VALUE
£245 million

SHORTLISTED

THE SURGERY
Hammersmith Bridge Road, London W6

GUY GREENFIELD ARCHITECTS

CLIENT
West London Health Estates

STRUCTURAL ENGINEER
Cooper Associates

SERVICES ENGINEER
KUT Partnership

CONTRACTOR
Benson

CONTRACT VALUE
£1.16 million

JUDGES

MARCO GOLDSCHMIED
Former RIBA President (chair)

WILL ALSOP
Architect, Stirling Prize winner in 2000 and shortlisted in 1997 and 1999

PAUL FINCH
Publisher of *The Architects' Journal*

ALICE RAWSTHORN
Director of the Design Museum

JANET STREET-PORTER
Journalist and broadcaster

2002

GATESHEAD MILLENNIUM BRIDGE
Gateshead, Tyne and Wear

WILKINSON EYRE ARCHITECTS

The harp-like structure of the Millennium Bridge seen at dusk from the Gateshead bank.

In 1997 Wilkinson Eyre won a competition to design a new foot-and-cycle crossing of the Tyne to link Gateshead with Newcastle. The brief called for a footbridge that met the ground on either riverbank; other bridges, because of the Tyne's steep gorge, do so further inland. This was likely to mean a steep gradient (or steps) if there was to be sufficient clearance even for small craft, making the bridge inaccessible to wheelchair users or any but the fittest cyclists. Wilkinson Eyre instead proposed a curved, longer deck to reduce the gradient. This in turn suggested a solution to the other part of

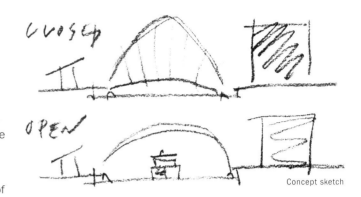

Concept sketch

the brief: a mechanism for allowing the occasional passage of larger river vessels. When it is in its lowered position, the bridge allows the same clearance as the Swing Bridge, some way upstream; and when raised, it gives the same 25-metre clearance as the massive Tyne Bridge. And it does so in spectacular fashion.

The idea is eminently simple: a pair of arches – one is the deck, the other supports the deck. Both arches pivot around their common springing point, allowing shipping to pass beneath. As the whole bridge tilts, it undergoes a metamorphosis into a grand arch, in an operation that evokes the slow opening of a huge eye. Viewed side on, when raised, it takes on the form of cupped hands or a human heart. Powerful images, all.

The wonder of this project speaks for itself, and the level of achievement is of the highest order. It started with the vision of the client and its decision to appoint Wilkinson Eyre Architects in partnership with the experienced bridge engineers Gifford and Partners. Every aspect of the bridge, from conception and detail through to execution, is simple and incredibly elegant.

In choosing the bridge as the winner, the Stirling judges described it as architecture and engineering in close harmony. Architecture, they said, is about the enclosure of space, and the bridge does just that because it moves. Its form certainly changes depending on where you are standing. And at night it looks like a sparkler describing shapes in the sky.

It is given to few pieces of architecture to have such a powerful social effect, not only providing a stimulus to regeneration but also helping to end the traditional enmity between Gateshead and Newcastle. Wilkinson Eyre's was the obvious solution to a new Tyne crossing: it was just that no one had ever thought of it before.

Left: The bridge seen from the newly landscaped approach on the Newcastle side.

Below: The curves of the arch and the deck frame Norman Foster's Sage Gateshead.

CLIENT
Gateshead Council

STRUCTURAL/SERVICES ENGINEER
Gifford and Partners

LIGHTING CONSULTANT
Jonathan Speirs & Associates

CONTRACTOR
Harbour & General

CONTRACT VALUE
£17.7 million

IMAGES
Tony Chapman (left); Doug Hall –
Bonney's News Agency (opposite);
Steve Mayes (below)

2002

SHORTLISTED

DANCE BASE
Grassmarket, Edinburgh

MALCOLM FRASER ARCHITECTS

CLIENT
Dance Base

STRUCTURAL ENGINEER
Cundall Johnston & Partners

SERVICES ENGINEER
K.J. Tait Engineers

THEATRE DESIGNER
Andrew Storer Designs

ACOUSTICS
New Acoustics

CONTRACTOR
HBG Construction

CONTRACT VALUE
£5 million

SHORTLISTED

DOWNLAND GRIDSHELL, WEALD AND DOWNLAND OPEN AIR MUSEUM
Chichester, West Sussex

EDWARD CULLINAN ARCHITECTS

CLIENT
Weald and Downland Open Air Museum

STRUCTURAL/SERVICES ENGINEER
Buro Happold

CONTRACTOR
E.A. Chiverton

CONTRACT VALUE
£1.6 million

SHORTLISTED

ERNSTING'S SERVICE CENTRE
Coesfeld-Lette, Germany

DAVID CHIPPERFIELD ARCHITECTS

CLIENT
Ernsting

STRUCTURAL ENGINEERS
Jane Wernick Associates with Arup Düsseldorf

SERVICES ENGINEER
Ingenieurbüro PGH

CONTRACTOR
E. Heitkamp

CONTRACT VALUE
£11.5 million

SHORTLISTED

HAMPDEN GURNEY CHURCH OF ENGLAND PRIMARY SCHOOL

Nutford Place, London W1

BUILDING DESIGN PARTNERSHIP

CLIENT
Hampden Gurney School

STRUCTURAL/SERVICES ENGINEER
Building Design Partnership

CONTRACTOR
Jarvis Construction

CONTRACT VALUE
£6 million

SHORTLISTED

LLOYD'S REGISTER OF SHIPPING

Fenchurch Street, London EC3

RICHARD ROGERS PARTNERSHIP

CLIENT
Lloyd's Register of Shipping

STRUCTURAL ENGINEER
Anthony Hunt Associates

SERVICES ENGINEER
Arup

CONTRACTOR
Sir Robert McAlpine

CONTRACT VALUE
£70 million

SHORTLISTED

MILLENNIUM WING, NATIONAL GALLERY OF IRELAND

Dublin, Ireland

BENSON + FORSYTH

CLIENT
The National Gallery of Ireland

STRUCTURAL ENGINEER
O'Connor Sutton Cronin

SERVICES ENGINEER
Oscar Faber

CONTRACTOR
Michael McNamara & Co.

CONTRACT VALUE
£10.7 million

JUDGES

PAUL HYETT
RIBA President (chair)

PAUL FINCH
Publisher of *The Architects' Journal*

WAYNE HEMINGWAY
Designer

KATE MOSSE
Novelist

FARSHID MOUSSAVI
Architect

2003

LABAN
Creekside, London SE8

HERZOG & DE MEURON

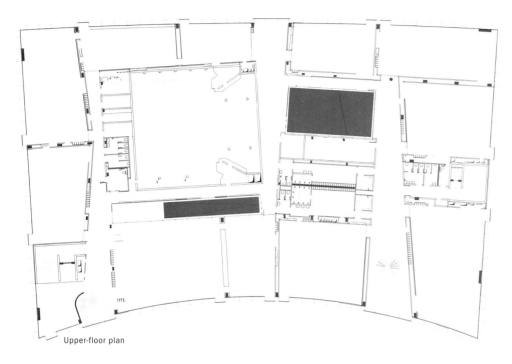

Upper-floor plan

Laban has given Deptford a significant and beautiful new landmark. The building is a singular and simple container with a double-skinned wall. The wall is constructed of a delicate external membrane of coloured polycarbonate panels, devised in collaboration with the artist Michael Craig-Martin, concealing a utilitarian energy-saving inner layer of insulation and translucent glass panels. At carefully considered moments, the inner and outer worlds are more immediately connected by ambiguously scaled, framed transparent panels.

The dance studios are pressed up against the external envelope, and utilize the exquisite coloured translucency of the walls to separate the plane of the timber floors from the massive ribbed-concrete soffits. The labyrinthine quality of the internal circulation is dramatized by the high chroma of the wall paint, darkly toned interiors, the interior light wells and, most dramatically, the sculptural gloss-black-painted spiral stairs, one at the front, the other at the rear. The creative and inspiring world of dance is matched by that of art and architecture.

Inside the space, there are ramps up towards studios and theatres, and down towards the café and treatment centres. All the activities of the dance centre are intermixed and distributed on two levels, promoting communication throughout this complex building. The project is inventive in the way its form reveals the choreography of movement. The public circulation spaces are full of wit in the curving handrail, which counters the hard line of the dance-studio bar.

'Laban will do for dance what Tate Modern has done for art', announces a screen inside the entrance to this less grandiloquent but equally eloquent building by the Swiss pair Herzog & de Meuron. And it is true: there is a creative buzz about the place that strikes you the moment you step inside. Throughout, the selection and detailing of materials provide a stunning luminance. The quality of light – both from the inside out and the outside in – is exceptionally beautiful for the occupiers, visitors and neighbours.

The judges thought this to be an extraordinarily fine building, one that raises the expectations of architecture in its engagement both with art forms and the local context. It makes a major contribution to the artistic life of the community while acting as a catalyst for the regeneration of the whole area.

It is a graceful building, generous in its relationship to its context: its reference to nearby St Paul's Church is geometrically precise, while it is calmly haphazard alongside the meandering Deptford Creek.

Above: The curved front elevation of polycarbonate filters soft light into the dance studios.

Opposite and right: Canvases for encounter and dance, the interiors are full of drama and incident.

CLIENT
Laban

STRUCTURAL/SERVICES ENGINEER
Whitbybird

THEATRE CONSULTANT
Carr & Angier

CONTRACTOR
Ballast Construction

CONTRACT VALUE
£14.4 million

IMAGES
Merlin Hendy

2003

SHORTLISTED

BEDZED
Wallington, Surrey

BILL DUNSTER ARCHITECTS

CLIENT
Dickon Robinson, The Peabody Trust

STRUCTURAL ENGINEER
Ellis & Moore

SERVICES ENGINEER
Arup

ENVIRONMENTAL CONSULTANT
BioRegional Development Group

CONTRACTOR
Gardiner & Theobald Construction Management

CONTRACT VALUE
£15 million

SHORTLISTED

30 FINSBURY SQUARE
London EC2

ERIC PARRY ARCHITECTS

CLIENTS
Scottish Widows with Jones Lang LaSalle

STRUCTURAL ENGINEER
Whitbybird

SERVICES ENGINEER
Hilson Moran Partnership

CONTRACTOR
HBG Construction

CONTRACT VALUE
£26 million

SHORTLISTED

THE GREAT COURT AT THE BRITISH MUSEUM
Great Russell Street, London WC1

FOSTER + PARTNERS

CLIENT
The British Museum

STRUCTURAL/SERVICES ENGINEER
Buro Happold

HISTORIC BUILDING ADVISERS
Giles Quarme & Associates; Caroe & Partners; Ian Bristow

CONTRACTOR
Mace

CONTRACT VALUE
£100 million

SHORTLISTED

PLYMOUTH THEATRE ROYAL PRODUCTION CENTRE
Plymouth, Devon

IAN RITCHIE ARCHITECTS

CLIENT
Plymouth Theatre Royal

STRUCTURAL/SERVICES ENGINEER
Arup

CONTRACTOR
Bluestone

CONTRACT VALUE
£5.8 million

SHORTLISTED

TREE SHELTER – AN TURAS
Tiree, Inner Hebrides

SUTHERLAND HUSSEY ARCHITECTS

CLIENT
Tiree Arts Enterprise

STRUCTURAL ENGINEER
David Narro Associates

ARTISTS
Jake Harvey; Sandra Kennedy; Glen Onwin; Donald Urquhart

CONTRACTOR
Inscape Joinery

CONTRACT VALUE
£95,000

JUDGES

GEORGE FERGUSON
RIBA President (chair)

ISABEL ALLEN
Editor of *The Architects' Journal*

JULIAN BARNES
Novelist

JUSTINE FRISCHMANN
Singer and TV presenter

CHRIS WILKINSON
Architect, Stirling Prize winner in 2001 and 2002, and shortlisted in 1997 and 1999

2004

Above and opposite, top: The distinctive shape makes this one of the most talked-about tall buildings in London, if not the world, but it is also key to its environmental strategy.

Opposite, bottom: A view down into one of the spiral voids that draw fresh air up through the building.

WINNER

30 ST MARY AXE
London EC3

FOSTER + PARTNERS

The client, Swiss Re, wanted a landmark building and it certainly got it from Foster + Partners. But it obtained not just a shiny new logo for its previously little-known reinsurance business; it also got a building that is loved by Londoners, the forty-storey tapering tower that is a popular icon on the city skyline.

The architects describe 30 St Mary Axe as 'the capital's first environmentally progressive tall building'. And indeed the scheme takes many of the ideas about naturally ventilated high-rises – such as drawing fresh air through the light wells that spiral up the building – from the same practice's Commerzbank in Frankfurt (shortlisted in 1998). These light wells are triangular on plan, and divide the otherwise continuous ring of offices on each floor into six segments. Each of these segments therefore benefits from being close to a pair of spiral voids.

What this complex three-dimensional geometry achieves for the building is both clever and intelligent. In addition to breaking up the office areas into well-proportioned chunks and providing atria and spatial interest, the light wells serve to bring light and air right into the depths of the building.

The architects have made the most of the benefits of the tapering volume at pedestrian level, too. Unlike in the earlier versions of this scheme, in which the building took up the whole site, the reduction in the building's girth at ground level allows for through routes, helping to knit the City back together. Also, the relatively small footprint of a circular building frees up additional precious ground space for landscaping. Low walls and seats marking the historic boundaries of the site (formerly the site of the Baltic Exchange) define a public plaza giving safe access to the double-height shops at ground-floor level. The aerodynamic form also means that there are fewer downdraughts than in the case of a rectilinear building, further increasing public comfort. Another effect of the tapering form is that, from close up, it is impossible to take in the whole of the building, so that the bulk one would usually associate with a 46,000-square-metre structure is greatly reduced.

Internally, the ground-floor lift lobby is suitably elegant, and the bar at the top of the building responds to the challenge and opportunity of elevation, situation and 360-degree views, making it one of the very best rooms in twenty-first-century London. At last, London is getting back the vantage points it richly deserves.

CLIENT
Swiss Re

STRUCTURAL ENGINEER
Arup

LIGHTING DESIGN
Speirs + Major

MAIN CONTRACTOR
Skanska Construction UK

CONTRACT VALUE
Confidential

IMAGES
Grant Smith – Foster + Partners
(opposite); Nigel Young – Foster +
Partners (left; below)

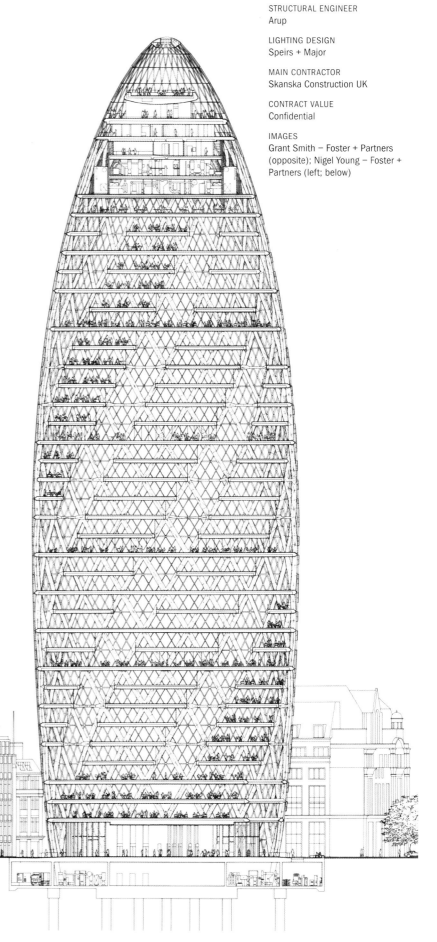

Section

61

2004

SHORTLISTED

THE BUSINESS ACADEMY BEXLEY
Erith, Kent

FOSTER + PARTNERS

CLIENT
Garrard Education Trust

SPONSORS
Sir David and Lady Garrard

STRUCTURAL ENGINEER
Buro Happold

CONTRACTOR
Exterior International

CONTRACT VALUE
Confidential

SHORTLISTED

IMPERIAL WAR MUSEUM NORTH
Trafford Wharf Road, Manchester

STUDIO DANIEL LIBESKIND

CLIENT
Trustees Imperial War Museum North

ASSOCIATE ARCHITECT
Leach Rhodes Walker

STRUCTURAL ENGINEER
Arup

SERVICES ENGINEER
Connell Mott MacDonald

EXHIBITION DESIGN
Real Studios

CONTRACTOR
Sir Robert McAlpine

CONTRACT VALUE
£19.7 million

SHORTLISTED

KUNSTHAUS
Graz, Austria

PETER COOK AND COLIN FOURNIER

CLIENT
Kunsthaus

LOCAL ARCHITECT
Architektur Consult

STRUCTURAL ENGINEER
Bollinger + Grohmann

SERVICES ENGINEER
HL-Technik Engineering

CONTRACTOR
SFL

CONTRACT VALUE
€40 million

SHORTLISTED

PHOENIX INITIATIVE
Coventry, West Midlands

MacCORMAC JAMIESON PRICHARD

CLIENT
Coventry City Council

EXECUTIVE ARCHITECT (PHASE II)
PCPT Architects

STRUCTURAL ENGINEERS
Babtie (Harris & Sutherland); Dewhurst Macfarlane & Partners;
Whitbybird

SERVICES ENGINEER
Michael Popper Associates

LANDSCAPE ARCHITECT
Rumney Design Associates

ART CONSULTANT
Vivien Lovell – Modus Operandi Art Consultants

ARTISTS
Alex Beleschenko; Chris Browne; Jochen Gerz; Susanna Heron;
David Morley; Françoise Schein; David Ward; Kate Whiteford

LIGHTING DESIGN
Speirs + Major

CONTRACTORS
Balfour Beatty; Butterley Construction; Galliford Try

CONTRACT VALUE
£50 million

SHORTLISTED

THE SPIRE
Dublin, Ireland

IAN RITCHIE ARCHITECTS

CLIENT
Dublin City Council

STRUCTURAL/SERVICES ENGINEER
Arup

CONTRACTOR
SIAC Radley Joint Venture

CONTRACT VALUE
£3.07 million

JUDGES

TED CULLINAN
Architect and Stirling Prize shortlisted in 2002
(chair)

ISABEL ALLEN
Editor of *The Architects' Journal*

DEBORAH BULL
Dancer

ANTONY GORMLEY
Sculptor

FRANCINE HOUBEN
Architect

WINNER

THE SCOTTISH PARLIAMENT
Horse Wynd, Edinburgh

EMBT AND RMJM

members' offices; and, above all, the chamber, which imbues the parliament with a sense of the country's long history.

The building is a statement of sparkling excellence. On the Memory Wall, one of the inscriptions reads, 'Say little and say it well.' This scheme is definitely saying a lot rather than little, but it certainly says it well.

John Gibbons explained the £200 million project over-run in pragmatic terms to the Stirling judges: 'The £40 million original quote was a political figure – what Dewar knew he could get the politicians to agree. It was never realistic for a new building. What's more, the brief has changed out of all recognition: the first figure was for an 11,000-square-metre building, basically just a chamber; the MSP's offices and so on take it to 33,000 square metres.'

The Scottish Parliament is a once-in-a-lifetime building, and it is refreshing that, for once with a British scheme, a decision was made to spend a lot of money well, instead of an inadequate amount badly. Charles Jencks has written of it: 'This building explores new territory for Scottish identity and for architecture. In the era of the iconic building, it creates an iconology of references to nature and the locale, using complex messages as a substitute for the one-liner.'

Left: The complex elevations of Scotland's parliament are reflected in aquatic landscaping designed to resemble the lochans in Holyrood Park.

Below: The cathedral-like undercroft forms the public entrance to the parliament.

The Scottish Parliament is a remarkable architectural statement that makes an enormous impact not only on visitors to the building but also on its users, who repeatedly move through a series of extraordinary spaces and their changing effects.

That a project outlived both its original client (Donald Dewar) and its principal architect (Enric Miralles) and still got built – and built well – is very much down to the vision and dogged determination of one man and one woman: chief architect at the Scottish Executive, John Gibbons, and Miralles's widow, the redoubtable Benedetta Tagliabue, who was determined that her husband's concept should not be diluted. But this is a team effort, too: every bit as much Gibbons's building as it is Dewar's; just as it is RMJM's every bit as much as it is EMBT's.

In its successful landscaping, the building makes an organic transition between the city and the drama of the surrounding Scottish countryside. But it is the internal public spaces that most impress: the crypt-like entrance hall; the committee rooms (possibly the most mature pieces of architecture in the whole dizzying complex); the monastic

The chamber has done much to imbue the Scottish nation with a sense of permanence and independence.

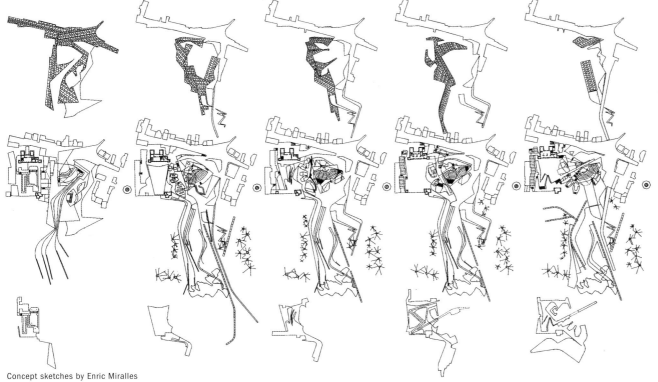

Concept sketches by Enric Miralles

CLIENT
The Scottish Parliamentary
Corporate Body

STRUCTURAL ENGINEER
Arup

SERVICES ENGINEER
RMJM Scotland

CONTRACTOR
Bovis Lend Lease

CONTRACT VALUE
£250 million

IMAGES
Keith Hunter

2005

SHORTLISTED

BMW CENTRAL BUILDING AND PLANT
Leipzig, Germany

ZAHA HADID ARCHITECTS

CLIENT
BMW Group, Munich

STRUCTURAL/SERVICES ENGINEERS
AGP Arge Gesamtplanung; Anthony Hunt Associates

CONTRACTORS
ARGE Rohbau; Wolff & Müller with OBAG

CONTRACT VALUE
€54 million

SHORTLISTED

FAWOOD CHILDREN'S CENTRE
Fawood Avenue, London NW10

ALSOP DESIGN

CLIENT
Stonebridge Housing Action Trust

STRUCTURAL ENGINEER
Adams Kara Taylor

CONTRACTOR
Durkan

CONTRACT VALUE
£2.3 million

SHORTLISTED

JUBILEE LIBRARY
Brighton, East Sussex

BENNETTS ASSOCIATES WITH LOMAX CASSIDY & EDWARDS

CLIENT
Brighton & Hove City Council

STRUCTURAL/CIVIL ENGINEER
SKM Anthony Hunt

SERVICES ENGINEER
Fulcrum Consulting

ARTISTS
Caroline Barton; Kate Malone; Georgia Russell

CONTRACTOR
Rok

CONTRACT VALUE
£8 million

SHORTLISTED

LEWIS GLUCKSMAN GALLERY
Cork, Ireland

O'DONNELL + TUOMEY

CLIENT
University College Cork

STRUCTURAL ENGINEER
Horgan Lynch

SERVICES ENGINEER
Arup

CONTRACTOR
P.J. Hegarty & Sons

CONTRACT VALUE
£7 million

SHORTLISTED

McLAREN TECHNOLOGY CENTRE
Woking, Surrey

FOSTER + PARTNERS

CLIENT
McLaren Group

STRUCTURAL ENGINEER
Arup

SERVICES ENGINEER
Schmidt Reuter

ENVIRONMENTAL ENGINEER
WSP Development

PLANNING AND LANDSCAPE
Terence O'Rourke

CONTRACTOR
Kier Build

CONTRACT VALUE
Confidential

JUDGES

JACK PRINGLE
RIBA President (chair)

ISABEL ALLEN
Editor of *The Architects' Journal*

JOAN BAKEWELL
Journalist and broadcaster

MAX FORDHAM
Environmental engineer

PIERS GOUGH
Architect

2006

WINNER

NEW AREA TERMINAL, BARAJAS AIRPORT
Madrid, Spain
**RICHARD ROGERS PARTNERSHIP
WITH ESTUDIO LAMELA**

SHORTLIST

BRICK HOUSE
London W2
CARUSO ST JOHN ARCHITECTS

EVELINA CHILDREN'S HOSPITAL
Westminster Bridge Road, London SE1
HOPKINS ARCHITECTS

IDEA STORE WHITECHAPEL
Whitechapel Road, London E1
ADJAYE ASSOCIATES

NATIONAL ASSEMBLY FOR WALES
Cardiff Bay, Cardiff
RICHARD ROGERS PARTNERSHIP

PHAENO SCIENCE CENTER
Wolfsburg, Germany
**ZAHA HADID ARCHITECTS AND MAYER
BÄHRLE FREIE ARCHITEKTEN BDA**

JUDGES

IAN RITCHIE
Architect and Stirling Prize shortlisted
in 1998, 2003 and 2004 (chair)

ISABEL ALLEN
Editor of *The Architects' Journal*

STEFAN BEHNISCH
Architect and Stirling Prize shortlisted
in 1998

MARIELLA FROSTRUP
Broadcaster

MARTHA SCHWARTZ
Landscape architect

15   158   157   156

WINNER

NEW AREA TERMINAL, BARAJAS AIRPORT
Madrid, Spain

RICHARD ROGERS PARTNERSHIP
WITH ESTUDIO LAMELA

CLIENT
AENA

STRUCTURAL ENGINEERS
Anthony Hunt Associates; TPS with
OTEP; HCA

FAÇADE ENGINEER
Arup

CONTRACTOR
UTE

CONTRACT VALUE
£1238 million

IMAGES
Amparro Garrido (opposite, top;
p. 74); Roland Halbe (opposite,
bottom; p. 72); Manuel Renau
(right; p. 73; p. 75)

Bamboo adds warmth to the ceilings of the check-in area, and extends outside to form the soffits of the wavy-profiled canopy.

At a time when it was already working on Heathrow's interminable Terminal 5 project, Richard Rogers's practice was appointed to design what is in effect a new airport for Madrid, more than doubling the capacity of the existing one. The Spanish airport was delivered while the British were still tied up in planning; so much for *mañana*. But the fact that the two projects ran concurrently meant that one could learn lessons from the other.

The sheer scale and complexity of what has been tackled and achieved in Madrid cannot be overestimated. The development was six years in construction. Particularly impressive are the extruded forms of the 1.2-km-long terminal and its 1-km-long satellite, linked by underground train and accommodating thirty-six and twenty-six stands respectively, handling up to 35 million passengers annually. Equally remarkable is the neat industrial aesthetic of the car park, with its 9000 spaces, as well as the integrated train and metro station in its cathedral-like housing, which completes the complex. So as to speed up proceedings for all, the routes taken by domestic and Schengen Treaty passengers are split from those using international flights.

Richard Rogers Partnership sought and found a new approach to airport design, one that put the needs of passengers before those of airlines and airport operators. In response to the key challenge, that of efficiently processing constantly changing passenger flows and the associated luggage handling, the architects produced a linear diagram in the form of a clear sequence of spectacular spaces for both departing and arriving passengers. The various stages

2006

Aficionados of Rogers's work look for meaning in the colours, since they were used in earlier projects to indicate different types of service. But here the colours provide decoration as well as a means of wayfinding: boarding passes are marked with a colour, and the passenger's route is instantly apparent as red gives way to orange, orange to yellow, yellow to green, and green to blue. The device is carried through to the external steel structure, giving the whole building a joyful but never wilful exuberance. Elsewhere, a restrained and functional approach is consistently applied to great effect, resulting in a visually clean, remarkably uncluttered and soothing environment.

The powerful wave-form of the elegant over-sailing roof is a unifying feature and succeeds in being both dominant and yet calmly and self-assuredly understated. The sinuous, lightweight consistency of the bamboo-slatted lining contrasts with the modular repetition of the gymnastic steel roof structure, which is in turn supported off a monumental concrete frame. The structure accommodates vast rooflights that provide shaded daylight throughout the upper level. Intentionally expressive air-conditioning outlets, resembling giant bar-code readers, animate the baggage-collection stands.

The building is robust enough to withstand the results of minor battles lost in terms of signage and shopping, the simplicity and clarity of the architectural ambition being dominant. Nowhere is this more evident than outside, where the now aluminium-clad roof again emerges as the defining feature, minimizing its impact by means of the overhanging long edges and recessed clear-glazed façades, cloaking the richness within and reinforcing the extruded nature of this

in the progression from check-in, through passport control and ever-more rigorous security procedures, to departure lounges with long views through the fully glazed façade to the mountains beyond, and finally to boarding, are articulated by means of 'floating' parallel linear floor planes, separated from one another by dramatic voids or natural light-filled canyons dramatically spanned by bridges. The accommodation is spread over six floors, so that departures and arrivals are clearly separated vertically. The three floors above ground deal with check-in, security, boarding and baggage reclaim; the floors below ground, with maintenance, baggage processing and the transfer of passengers between buildings.

KEY

Airside passengers

Vertical and horizontal circulations

Retail

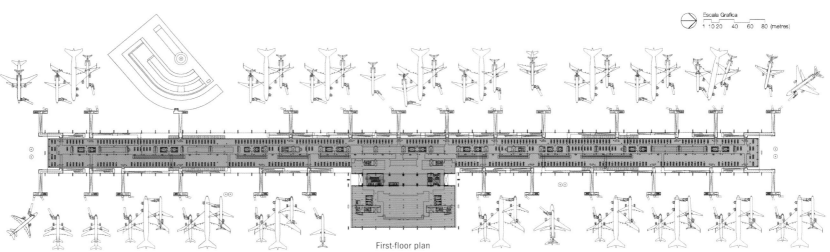

Escala Grafica
1 10 20   40   60   80 (metres)

First-floor plan

The use of colour – not just for decoration, but also for reasons of utility – has always been a signature of Richard Rogers.

2006

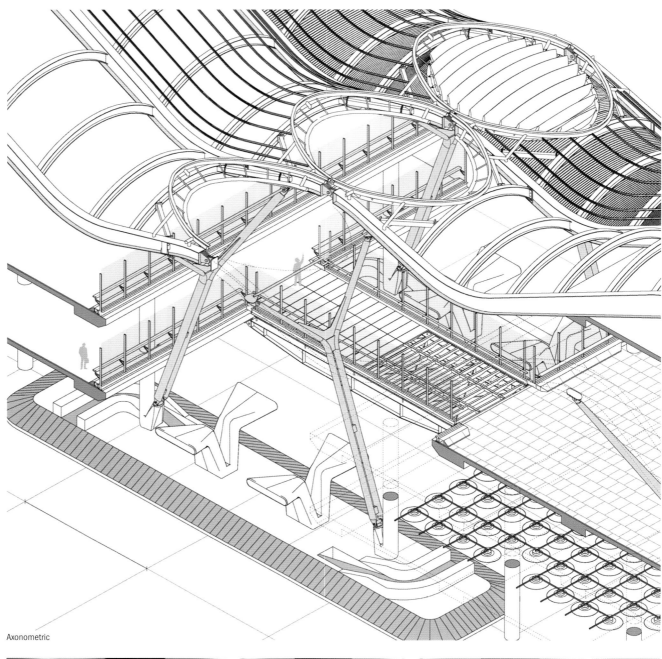

Axonometric

Balancing daylight and natural light is key in airport design to reducing passengers' stress levels.

infinitely extendable tour de force of an airport. Barajas restores much of the joy and excitement of flight that has been altogether lost in recent years.

Looking back at the Barajas project in 2015, Ivan Harbour, the director in charge, said: 'We had been working on Terminal 5 for seven years when we won Barajas, and we had looked at a number of strategies for how you might organize a terminal at that scale. A terminal has to work well. The flows are really important: the time it takes to transfer from plane to plane, the time it takes to wait for your bags; these things are absolutely essential. If we can get them right, the architects succeed in making it a pleasant place to be. This is an enormous terminal; it's such a big thing that we couldn't conceive of it as one entity. At the competition stage we took the decision that we needed to design one part well and repeat it many times. And so we can focus on that, and do it very well.'

2006

BRICK HOUSE
London W2

CARUSO ST JOHN ARCHITECTS

The fractal geometries are highlighted by holes punched through the concrete, creating mood with light and shade.

This new house is on an awkward back-land site that is shaped like a horse's head, and is overlooked by taller houses on three sides. Planning restrictions dictated what is effectively a single-storey above-ground building, so as not to steal the neighbours' daylight. The new house is accessed through an archway at the end of a west London street. The Victorian entrance contrasts with the modern, austere, rendered corridor that forms the gently rising route into the house. The very limited palette of brick and concrete has been carefully detailed to create an outstanding piece of modern architecture. The result is a tribute to the determination of both architect and client.

This is a brave, intelligent and original study in the use of ordinary materials, developed in both a simple and sculptural way. The ceiling concrete is raw and coarse; where most architects would have chosen a smooth, creamy mix for an exposed soffit in a domestic setting, Caruso St John has selected a concrete that is definitely more Queen Elizabeth Hall than National Theatre. Further, the bold fractal geometries of the ceiling on the upper floor might seem

gestural to some, given that domestic context, but the varied heights and angles help to define the functional use of the spaces beneath them: a low horizontal ceiling over the dining area; a high, domed profile over the main sitting area. All bedrooms are at lower-ground level, overlooking small courtyard gardens that complete the geometry of the rooms they serve. In fact, the shape of the site has informed the shapes of all rooms – one bedroom is triangular. Occupying the upper floor, at raised ground-floor level, are the main living space, incorporating dining and kitchen areas in one volume, and a separate study-cum-TV room. The warmth and subtlety of the interiors throughout are highly impressive, likewise the varying planes and the use of light.

Externally, it reads as an entirely different house, partly on account of the site, but partly because the skin gives no clue to the innovation within. The use of a single material, brick, in which to wrap the house is masterful and all but inevitable. The architects have likened the scheme, hidden behind a Victorian façade, to a baroque chapel locked up behind a Roman street. This is by no means a fanciful conceit.

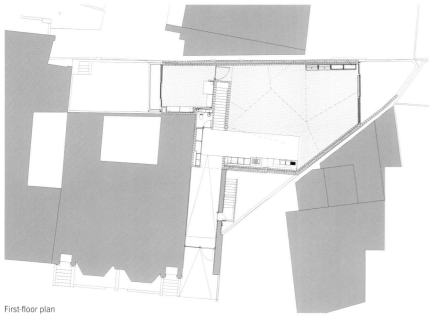

First-floor plan

CLIENT
Private

STRUCTURAL ENGINEER
Price & Myers

SERVICES ENGINEER
Mendick Waring

CONTRACTOR
Harris Calnan Construction

CONTRACT VALUE
Confidential

IMAGES
Hélène Binet (opposite);
Ioana Marinescu (above)

SHORTLISTED

EVELINA CHILDREN'S HOSPITAL
Westminster Bridge Road, London SE1

HOPKINS ARCHITECTS

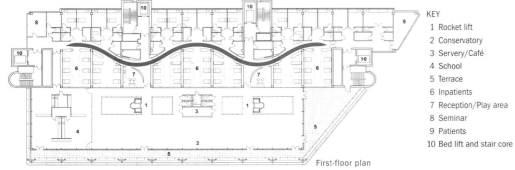

KEY
1 Rocket lift
2 Conservatory
3 Servery/Café
4 School
5 Terrace
6 Inpatients
7 Reception/Play area
8 Seminar
9 Patients
10 Bed lift and stair core

First-floor plan

Part of the developing plan for the St Thomas' Hospital campus, the Evelina Children's Hospital stands out as a beacon of optimism. Hopkins won the job through an RIBA competition in 1999; the project was well worth the wait. This is a hospital where the patient, not the institution, is given priority.

This is Hopkins's first hospital, but the practice's inexperience is by no means the constraint it might at first appear. It means that the architects are not hidebound by experience and the caution that can attend it, and they are freed from the preconceptions of regular practitioners in the field. In fact, their very innocence was one reason the client fell for their scheme. And they fulfilled the imaginative brief, which was to come up with 'a hospital that does not feel like a hospital'. They have rethought the building type, bringing to the process their experience of commercial, education and performance buildings. The result is a surprisingly open structure, not only in the form of the gigantic conservatory, which is overlooked by the wards, but also in the wards themselves, which open internally on to a serpentine corridor. The atrium is really a vast greenhouse the size of a football pitch. The only two permanent uses of this space are a café and a school, which is placed at one end, its rooms defined by screens.

An entrance on Lambeth Palace Road, reached by a wheelchair- and pram-friendly ramp, stands at one end of an internal street that is illuminated by shafts of light from the spectacular atrium above. While the building is impeccably organized, the emphasis of the design is on providing an environment in which children feel comfortable and relaxed. The technical facilities, normally so associated with fear, are made pleasant and inviting; the shared play areas and the school are planned to be visible and inviting to newcomers and visitors; and daylight reaches every hospital bed. Instead of the usual grim institutional corridors, a colourful, gently winding path links the small wards. (Orthogonal geometries are reserved for the serious business of operating, intensive care and recovery.)

Evelina will not solve all the problems faced by the National Health Service in its massive building and refurbishment programme – it was largely funded by a charitable trust, which is how it could avoid the PFI route – but there are plenty of lessons here, not just for architects, but also for health administrators and politicians.

CLIENT
Evelina Children's Hospital

STRUCTURAL ENGINEER
Buro Happold

SERVICES ENGINEER
Hoare Lea

CONTRACTOR
M.J. Gleeson

CONTRACT VALUE
£41.8 million

IMAGES
Paul Tyagi – VIEW

The atrium is the unifying device of
the hospital, not just letting in light
but also producing generous, less-
programmed spaces for patients.

2006

IDEA STORE WHITECHAPEL
Whitechapel Road, London E1

ADJAYE ASSOCIATES

The idea of the Idea Store is to make the library a part of the community. The ivory tower has become one of glass, taking its scale from the nearby hospital, sorting office and old brewery. But its colourful character, a striped motif of green and blue glazed interlayers, echoes the awnings of the market stalls of the Whitechapel Road that press up against the building.

The Idea Store represents a new departure for public buildings. It is both civic and inclusive, iconic and contextual, but, most importantly, it is popular and loved by its users. Its civic character comes from its height and the boldness of a façade that hangs precariously over the pavement and those market stalls. Its inclusiveness comes from its situation right in the heart of the community it serves. Customers can drop in en route from the supermarket to the market. Two entrances welcome them in to a ground floor that accommodates a familiar and unthreatening video store and a children's library. Instead of placing the café here, the clients and architects agreed to adopt the shopping-mall principle of the anchor store and use the café to draw people through the building and up to the top floor. It must be one of best new public rooms in London, with stunning views towards the City.

In old money, this is a library, but its being dubbed an 'idea store' is more than an exercise in rebranding. It is an accurate representation of the building's mixed activities, which include nursery, dance studio, seminar spaces, internet facilities, a large external deck and physiotherapy training classrooms, as well as the library itself.

Fully glazed buildings require the scheme to work harder in energy-saving terms by producing other benefits – here, the interaction with the Whitechapel community.

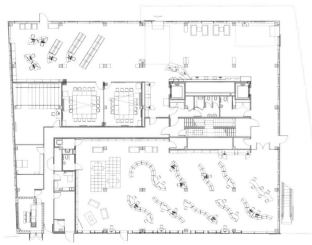

Ground-floor plan

The glazed façade is hung from deep timber mullions that support the shelving and accommodate seating and desk space. The interiors are also distinctive on account of the careful placement and specification of the furniture and zigzag shelving, designed by the architects themselves, and the deep-red rubber floor. Exposed structural concrete fins in the ceiling act as a backdrop to the bespoke strip lighting, the design of which mirrors the patterns of the shelves.

Most new libraries in Britain are being procured through PFI, under which good design is frequently eroded or institutionalized. The Idea Store shows that ambitious clients picking adventurous architects and putting them to work in a traditional manner is still to best way to make good buildings.

CLIENT
London Borough of Tower Hamlets

STRUCTURAL ENGINEER
Arup

CONTRACTOR
William Verry

CONTRACT VALUE
£12 million

IMAGES
Lyndon Douglas (opposite);
Timothy Soar (right, above and top)

2006

NATIONAL ASSEMBLY FOR WALES
Cardiff Bay, Cardiff

RICHARD ROGERS PARTNERSHIP

The simple elegance of the competition-winning entry: a Miesian glass box under a wave-form roof and atop a flight of steps leading up from the bay has brilliantly survived a process almost as complex as Zaha Hadid's ill-fated Cardiff Opera House next door. The result is an exceptional public building, and its democratic function is clearly expressed. From across the water, the debating chamber is revealed above the upper foyer space through fully glazed façades. Low slate walls define a series of accessible terraces overlooking the bay.

It is a delight to see children and parents casually peppered around the spectacular upper foyer under the flowing cedar-clad ceiling, enjoying the illusion that they are inside a beautifully honed musical instrument. This is the most impressive feature: pre-curved laths of western red cedar are fixed over an angular steel frame, giving the building its organic character, both inside and externally on the soffit of the shade-giving canopy.

Once through the inevitable security checks, visitors have the right to roam and take in the processes of government at work: to peek into the debating chamber or the committee and meeting rooms (all daylit by two canyons that run the length of the building); to take one of the 128 seats (12 for wheelchair users) in the glazed-in public viewing gallery in the chamber; or to have coffee in the café bar at the oriel (upper) level. The circular debating chamber is placed at the heart of the building. A glazed lantern allows daylight to penetrate, while a roof cowl rotates with the wind to drive the natural ventilation. Internally, the roof sweeps up in a dramatic bell form, finished in concentric aluminium rings, with a glazed lantern above. A conical mirror suspended inside the lantern reflects more light into the chamber.

There has clearly been a strong desire from the team for the building to meet a high level of environmental

KEY
1 Debating chamber
2 Committee rooms
3 Meeting rooms/Offices
4 Public gallery
5 Upper foyer

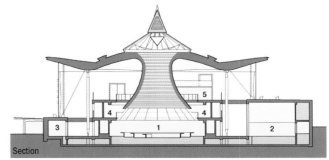

Section

objectives, with the result that it has been awarded a BREEAM (Building Research Establishment Environmental Assessment Method) rating of 'Excellent'. The materials were thoroughly reviewed in terms of their embodied energy and 100-year-plus design life. Such techniques as biomass boilers, ground-source heat pumps and water harvesting have resulted in a largely naturally ventilated building, with a mixed-mode system available to the debating chamber, public gallery and committee rooms.

CLIENT
National Assembly for Wales

STRUCTURAL ENGINEER
Arup

LANDSCAPE ARCHITECT
Gillespies

ENVIRONMENTAL CONSULTANT
BDSP Partnership

CONTRACTOR
Taylor Woodrow

CONTRACT VALUE
£40,997 million

IMAGES
Richard Bryant – Arcaid

2006

SHORTLISTED

PHAENO SCIENCE CENTER
Wolfsburg, Germany

ZAHA HADID ARCHITECTS AND MAYER BÄHRLE FREIE ARCHITEKTEN BDA

'Phaeno' relates to the idea of embodying or manifesting something, in this case scientific concepts – and even Zaha Hadid's soaring spaces struggle to compete for the attention of children of all ages with the scientific experiments and games that fill the place. For architects, this building is another kind of manifestation. It is the embodiment, in the form of a major public project, of work that many of us have experienced only in paintings, drawings and pavilions. It is fascinating to visit a building that is the realization of an imaginative world that we know vividly through twenty years of abstract images. Hadid had been pushing at the edges of architecture for a long time, but the experimentation had been done mainly on-screen. Then, in Strasbourg, Cincinnati, Leipzig and here in Wolfsburg, her extraordinary conceptions were dragged into screaming and mewling life. This revolutionary building lets us experience space in ways that never before seemed possible.

At first sight, the Science Center is an object of mystery, a kind of undulating earthwork. There is an undercroft, a dark grotto carved out of looming dreamlike forms, like London's Southbank Centre, only even better. The structural engineers,

Adams Kara Taylor, were crucial to the realization of the scheme. Innovative technical solutions were required for the conical supports that raise the building off the ground and create the undercroft. The final dramatic result was achieved not by columns and beams but by means of self-compacting concrete, making Phaeno the largest building in Europe to have been constructed in this way.

Doorways carved out of the concrete lead the visitor up to an echoing barn full of gesticulating exhibits, most of which are at child height. The architects describe the building as a visitation from a future warp-world. What is strange for the visitor is that it is weirdly reminiscent of many other buildings, all at once: the sensuous board-marked supports of Le Corbusier's Unité d'Habitation, a 1960s steel diagrid space-frame, a baroque grotto. Even the windows look as though they have been lifted from passing commuter trains. There is something almost Joycean in the babble of collaged constructional languages. The point of a building such as this is that it should be like a beacon, illuminating a possible future. In fact, it is at heart an experiment, at one moment swashbuckling, at another gangling. At its best it is primitive.

KEY
1 Landscape
2 Shop
3 Workshop
4 Main entrance
5 Group entrance
6 Bistro
7 Auditorium
8 Laboratory/Loading
9 Event space
10 Coffee bar
11 Ramp to bridge
12 Access to parking

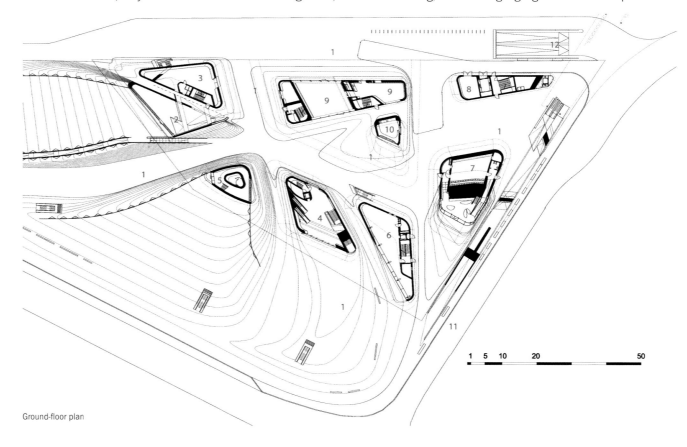

Ground-floor plan

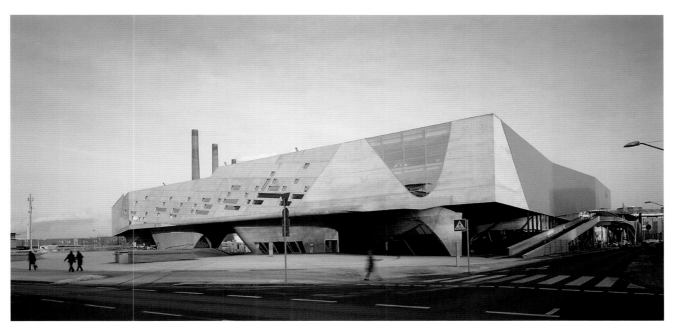

CLIENT
Phaeno Science Center

STRUCTURAL ENGINEERS
Adams Kara Taylor (UK); Tokarz
Frerichs Leipold (Germany)

SERVICES ENGINEERS
Buro Happold (UK); NEK (Germany)

CONTRACT VALUE
€40 million

IMAGES
Hélène Binet (left; below);
Richard Bryant – Arcaid (opposite)

Opposite: This a museum for children, but many of the exhibits are designed to make use of the cavernous spaces.

Above and left: The elephantine structure is made a thing of beauty by the fluidity of Hadid's lines.

2007

WINNER

MUSEUM OF MODERN LITERATURE
Marbach am Neckar, Germany
DAVID CHIPPERFIELD ARCHITECTS

SHORTLIST

CASA DA MÚSICA
Porto, Portugal
OMA

DRESDEN STATION REDEVELOPMENT
Dresden, Germany
FOSTER + PARTNERS

THE SAVILL BUILDING
Windsor Great Park, Surrey
GLENN HOWELLS ARCHITECTS

VELES E VENTS, AMERICA'S CUP BUILDING
Valencia, Spain
DAVID CHIPPERFIELD ARCHITECTS

YOUNG VIC THEATRE
The Cut, London SE1
HAWORTH TOMPKINS

JUDGES

SUNAND PRASAD
RIBA President (chair)

TOM BLOXHAM
Property developer

ALAIN DE BOTTON
Writer and philosopher

LOUISA HUTTON
Architect and Stirling Prize shortlisted
in 2000

KIERAN LONG
Editor of *The Architects' Journal*

2007

WINNER

MUSEUM OF MODERN LITERATURE
Marbach am Neckar, Germany

DAVID CHIPPERFIELD ARCHITECTS

CLIENT
Deutsches Literaturarchiv Marbach

STRUCTURAL ENGINEER
Ingenieurgruppe Bauen

SERVICES ENGINEERS
Jaeger, Mornhinweg + Partner;
Burrer & Deuring Ingenieurbüro

SITE SUPERVISION
Wenzel + Wenzel

CONTRACT VALUE
€11.8 million

IMAGES
Jörg von Bruchhausen (p. 93); Julia
Magenau (p. 92 top and bottom);
Christian Richters – VIEW (opposite;
p. 90; p. 91; p. 92 centre)

Since the end of the Second World War, Germany more than any other country has been sensitive to matters concerning the neoclassical in architecture. This is not to suggest that the new museum is overtly classical, but rather that, had this scheme been submitted in a competition a decade or two earlier, it would almost certainly have been eliminated for its manner and formality. It is therefore encouraging that, with time, more purely architectural criteria have obtained in the making of such decisions, and that this fine project has been realized in commemoration of twentieth- and twenty-first-century German literature. As such, it celebrates the positives in recent German history.

Prior to reunification, the texts of various well-known German authors had been dispersed to East and West; they have now been brought together in this new museum. In a suitably commemorative manner, the building forms a small acropolis attached to the National Schiller Museum on a ridge overlooking the valley of the River Neckar.

The entrance sequence is simply brilliant. The visitor crosses an open terrace, negotiates a series of shallow steps into the generous portal formed in the colonnade, then enters the museum through giant hardwood doors. A staircase descends into a lobby, the secondary function of which is to allow the architect to demonstrate his mastery of detail: the impeccably matched veneers, the quality of the concrete, the over-scaled doors. Other detailing includes the

alarm buttons recessed into concrete of the kind architects almost want to lick; and the use of a tough yet sensuous felt on the seats in the lecture theatre and in the loggias.

It is at the moment of descent that the building shows its pedigree – a sense of a progression to somewhere beyond, combined with a fine but selective palette of materials and subdued top-lighting. The route concludes in the permanent collection, where glass cases containing original manuscripts form a magical flickering landscape.

This is a building that is simultaneously rich and restrained, a trick Chipperfield pulls off as well as any architect working today. The control and discrimination in the choice of materials have by now become a signature of the practice, but above all it is in the handling of the 'difficult whole' that the building excels.

Marbach could be described as a temple to literature; however, the architects are reluctant to use the term – though they do fall back on it occasionally as a useful shorthand. On approach, it certainly looks like a temple: a single-storey structure crowning a bluff above the valley. But segue around it, and as the land falls away it becomes a two-storey building. Part of the colonnade is blind, in-filled with concrete panels where there are galleries and with glass where there are offices or curating areas. The building plays such tricks continually. In the upper element, the columns support the corners; in the lower part, they stop short of the corners.

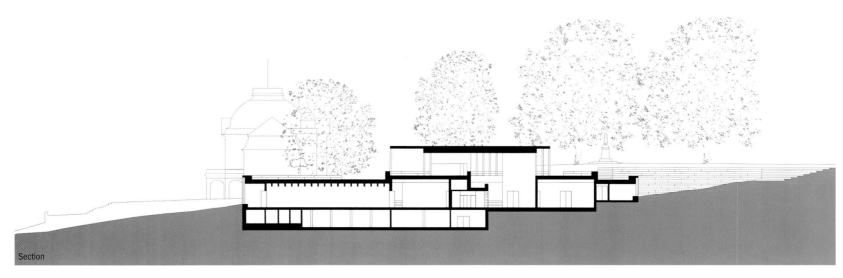

Section

The stripped-down classicism may seem unexceptional in the UK, but in Germany it sends a message that architecture can transcend history.

The minimal take on the neoclassical colonnade has become a feature of David Chipperfield's work, never better done than here at the Museum of Modern Literature.

2007

Internally, what at first sight is a simple circulation pattern in fact provides a series of alternative routes as the galleries and breakout areas interconnect. The former are all about pinpoint low-energy LED lighting (safe for the most delicate of manuscripts); the latter are flooded with sudden daylight and, because of the topography, captured views.

At just £2180 per square metre, this is a remarkably low-cost scheme in a high-cost country. The architects have made a merit of the need for economies. You can see that every penny spent has been carefully considered, and also that the right way to do things has always been chosen over the cheapest. It is a matter of thought and decision-making. The same local limestone that is used for all the inside and colonnaded floors is crushed to make the aggregate for a concrete that forms the columns and the outside floors. This is a well-ordered building, but a highly sensual one, too.

Speaking at the time he won the 2011 Royal Gold Medal, Chipperfield said: 'As architects, we like to talk about a lot of things, but we really don't like to talk about why a building looks the way it does. And if you ask somebody, "Why does your building look like that?", you'll get all sorts of reasons. It will be about structure, it will be about circulation, it will be about materiality, it will be about distinguishing itself. But we've spent modernism trying to avoid the issue. Form follows function; it looks like that because that's what it is. What a load of rubbish. In a way, it became a polemicized thing; either it's historical or it's new, and we've never really looked at the idea that modern architecture could represent some sort of continuity.'

The simple internal palette of raw concrete and walnut makes the perfect backdrop for display.

2007

CASA DA MÚSICA
Porto, Portugal

OMA

Level 1 plan

CLIENTS
Porto 2001 SA; Casa da Música

STRUCTURAL ENGINEERS
Arup; AFA Consultores

SERVICES ENGINEERS
Arup; AFA Consultores; RGA

ACOUSTICS
TNO; DHV

CONTRACTORS
Somague; Mesquita

CONTRACT VALUE
€100 million

IMAGES
OMA (right); Philippe Ruault
(opposite)

The Casa da Música looks as if it has been hammered into the ground, creating eruptions and ripples in an empty plaza, and providing a three-dimensional landscape for skateboarding, promenading and performance. This is a building that, surprisingly perhaps, arises directly out of its programme. The acousticians argued for an orthogonal shape for the concert hall (there are two halls, in fact), since this is the best shape in which to make and listen to music. The double-skin end walls of sinuous corrugated glass provide both acoustic enclosure and dramatically distorted views to the outside.

Having determined the shapes of the concert halls, the architects had to decide on the envelope. This was suggested by an unexecuted design for a house that OMA's Rem Koolhaas had always wanted to realize. Here, scaled up, it allowed an intriguing pattern of circulation, foyers, bars and breakout areas to develop between, as it were, the core and the shell. By sloping inwards at its base, the form initially repels efforts to get inside, but a wide staircase emerges through a canted slot and draws the visitor upwards and into this magic box of tricks. It is a building full of scenographic moments and ironic gestures. It feels as if the cranked form and twisting stairs should lead you around and over the auditorium, connecting and completing a special sequence. In fact, the two staircases remain separate: you are always on either the north or the south side of the building.

The clients selected Koolhaas from a shortlist that included Dominique Perrault and Norman Foster partly because of his interest in finding new uses for materials. Hence the alloy floors in reception, concert hall and stairs; the lace acoustic curtains; the ETFE pillows above the stage that reflect the musicians' sound; and, most dramatically, the 2-cm-thick, acoustically insulated rippled glass.

A visit to this building is an episodic, almost staccato experience. The tour is punctuated by strange moments. The VIP room is lined with blue patterned tiles, with one fully glazed wall high over the city – a contemporary Dutch take on a Portuguese tradition. A star dressing room has a fully glazed wall inclined as if to emphasize a voyeuristic connection to the plaza just below. This well-made building is intriguing, disquieting and dynamic, and fulfils another contemporary role as a strange, enigmatic and compelling object in the city of Porto.

2007

DRESDEN STATION REDEVELOPMENT
Dresden, Germany

FOSTER + PARTNERS

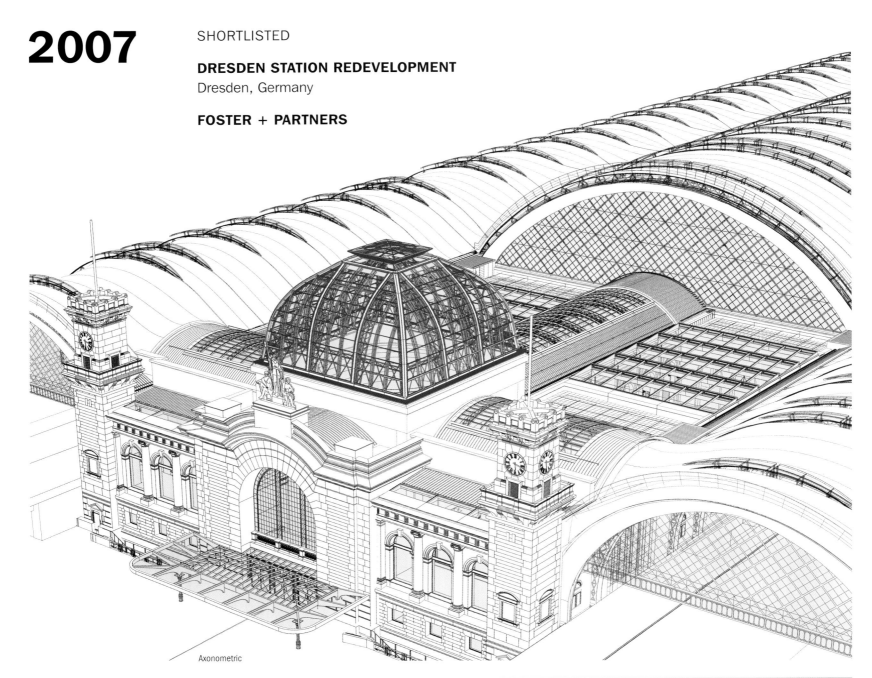

Axonometric

CLIENT
Deutsche Bahn

STRUCTURAL ENGINEERS
Buro Happold; Schmitt Stumpf
Frühauf und Partner

SERVICES ENGINEERS
Schmidt Reuter; Zibell Willner
& Partner

HISTORIC BUILDING ADVISER
ADB

CONTRACTOR
Deutsche Bahn Station & Service

CONTRACT VALUE
€146.6 million

IMAGES
Nigel Young – Foster + Partners

Opposite and below: The reworked cupola, over the intersection of the two arcades, has a moveable transparent foil cushion that allows warm air to flow up through the louvres.

Bottom: The 29,000-square-metre, three-vaulted roof has a taut skin of Teflon-coated fibreglass fabric stretched over the restored elaborate wrought-iron structure.

Opened in 1898, Dresden's main station, with its cruciform plan and lofty vaults, is a cathedral to the railway age. Foster + Partners' key move is one of apparent simplicity, but it belies a complexity that is both surprising and highly effective. The configuration of the station is not uncommon in Germany: elevated raised tracks and platforms for through trains on either side of low-level platforms and tracks for terminating ones. This suggested the grand entrance opening on to a public plaza, across which trams sweep, taking on and dropping off passengers. Observed from the high-level platforms, the scheme is a grand piece of theatre.

Although not totally destroyed by Allied bombing during the infamous aerial raids on Dresden in February 1945, the station was badly damaged and suffered further from unsympathetic repair and alterations. In fact, it probably suffered more at the hands of the East German Communist regime than it did at those of the British RAF. The appointment of British architects was magnanimous and appropriate. Foster + Partners won the competition on the strength of its proposal to re-roof the damaged late-nineteenth-century train shed with a lightweight fabric roof instead of reproducing the heavy timber-and-glass roof that had existed previously. This allowed a gentle touch to the repair of the steelwork, as well as providing more natural light. However, it is the aesthetic effect that is chiefly remarkable, for both the fine quality of the diffused light through the white fabric roof and for its formal qualities. In place of the parallel linear roofs and gutters of the original, the new fabric is pulled tightly down into the springing points of the arches in alternate bays, forming a fan vault somewhat reminiscent of that of King's College Chapel in Cambridge.

A similar approach has been adopted in the remaining inner courtyards, one hollowed as a food court. Here, the architects have exposed and simply cleaned the brick. That is the principle successfully applied throughout: to expose and repair the original where it remains, and where it does not – in the case of the staircases, for instance – to insert clean, modern elements. It is a technique that worked well in the Reichstag, after all.

This was a hugely complex job of conservation, and the station was kept open throughout – an achievement in itself. Dresden has a station of which it can once again be proud.

2007

THE SAVILL BUILDING
Windsor Great Park, Surrey

GLENN HOWELLS ARCHITECTS

Concept sketch

Opposite: The structure was assembled *in situ* over a flat scaffold deck. Adjustable props were then manipulated up and down until the roof achieved its final 3D form.

Below: The joinery was made by the same carpenters, the Green Oak Carpentry Company, that worked on the building's precursor, Ted Cullinan's Downland Gridshell (shortlisted in 2002).

This project is a good modern interpretation of that great British traditional form: the pavilion in the park. The Savill Building takes the form of a dramatic gridshell structure – albeit not a solely self-supporting one – made of timber from the park in which it sits. This innovative use of traditional materials means that the building harmonizes well with a skyline of mature trees. Burying it partially underground also helped to make it unobtrusive.

It is tough to make great architecture of a visitor centre. This one sits in a site of Special Scientific Interest, a Grade I-listed garden in the green belt. The client wanted a landmark. What it got is an appropriate response in a modern idiom, and it is delighted. The roof takes a distinctive undulating shape, which from a distance appears to float above the meadow on the entrance side of the building. Within the public area there are three main forms: the roof, which ripples over everything, the timber gridshell twisting and turning like bones beneath an animal's skin; a curving brick wall to the south, which runs through the building and extends beyond it to slope neatly into the adjoining folds in the landscape; and a glazed screen on the north face.

A gridshell from Glenn Howells is something of a turn-up for the books, as the firm is better known for its concrete-framed buildings. The decision to opt for a gridshell was by no means ideological; rather, it arose as the most appropriate solution to the problem of building in a sensitive parkland setting. Bringing in the help of an expert in the field, Buro Happold (which worked with Frei Otto and subsequently Ted Cullinan), Howells has taken the building form forward, adapting it to the needs of a twenty-first-century client.

Howells compares the building, not as immodestly as it might at first appear, to a medieval cathedral. He is not referring to the soaring spaces (though he might), but to the primacy of craft in the delivery of the project. It is about collaboration between all the professions and trades: architects, engineers, planners, carpenters, bricklayers, glaziers and, of course, a great client, all working together to produce a building that really is of a piece with its setting.

CLIENT
The Crown Estate

STRUCTURAL ENGINEERS
Buro Happold; Engineers HRW

SERVICES ENGINEER
Atelier Ten

JOINERY
The Green Oak Carpentry Company

CONTRACTOR
William Verry

CONTRACT VALUE
£5 million

IMAGES
Warwick Sweeney

2007

VELES E VENTS, AMERICA'S CUP BUILDING
Valencia, Spain

DAVID CHIPPERFIELD ARCHITECTS

Axonometric

Veles e Vents ('Sails and Winds'), the central base for all America's Cup teams and sponsors in Valencia, opened in May 2006, within a remarkable eleven months of the architects receiving the design commission. The building and park were designed to be the social focal point of the world's premier offshore racing competition, which was being staged in Europe for the first time in more than 150 years. This 10,000-square-metre shifting stack of wide trays or decks has an immediate appeal, combining the formal tension of its scale and asymmetry with the sheer modernist simplicity of white concrete, expanses of timber decking and white-painted steel trim. The shaded floor-slabs create, from improbably cantilevered viewing decks, 360-degree views of the industrial port, the new park and the offshore racing courses. The building is also the centrepiece of the reorganized old industrial port of Valencia. Cleverly planned, it manages to have no back or front and

The tray-like forms are unique in the Chipperfield *oeuvre*, and make the building a suitably populist one.

to feel open and easy, while providing all the necessary enclosures for services and circulation.

David Chipperfield does not normally do icons, yet this one literally put his practice on the map: he is rather proud of the fact that local city plans mark the 'edificio Chipperfield'. The concrete-framed building takes the form of three trays clad in nautical white-painted steel. Each tray is of different dimensions and not aligned with the one above, giving the scheme the look of a busy waiter struggling to balance his dishes. The effect lends a playfulness to what could have been a highly formal structure. In some ways, the eleven-month gestation and delivery period shows in the build quality, especially in the unforgiving salt air, but it has also led to benefits: it focused minds and meant that decisions were made quickly. Chipperfield says you can do anything if people – and he means clients and contractors – make up their minds and stick to decisions.

What has been achieved is truly remarkable: a pavilion for rich people and their hangers-on, yes, but, true to the architect's democratic principles, one that all Valencians can visit to use the bars and restaurants, which remain in full swing in the downtime between racing yachts and racing cars (Valencia was scheduled to host the America's Cup again in 2009 and also a series of Formula One Grands Prix).

CLIENT
Consorcio Valencia 2007

ASSOCIATE ARCHITECT
b720 Arquitectos

STRUCTURAL ENGINEER
Boma

SERVICES ENGINEER
Grupotec

CONTRACTOR
Ute Foredeck

CONTRACT VALUE
€36 million

IMAGES
Christian Richters – VIEW (opposite);
Richard Walch (above)

2007

YOUNG VIC THEATRE
The Cut, London SE1

HAWORTH TOMPKINS

CLIENT
The Young Vic Theatre Company

STRUCTURAL ENGINEER
Jane Wernick Associates

SERVICES ENGINEER
Max Fordham

CONTRACT VALUE
£6.9 million

CONTRACTOR
Willam Verry

IMAGES
Philip Vile

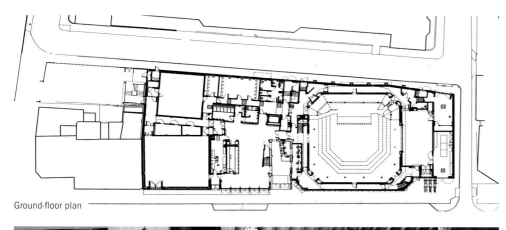

Ground-floor plan

The Cut is a cheerfully scruffy part of south London into which, in the 1970s, architect Bill Howell introduced the Young Vic at a cost of a mere £60,000. Times and prices change, but here Haworth Tompkins has remained true to the original while radically expanding opportunities for actors to make theatre and for audiences to enjoy it. The ad hoc aesthetic very much remains in the redesign, which has also retained the affection of local people. This is their theatre. The Young Vic has always encouraged experimental work, and its new building is suitably experimental.

The key result of the fruitful collaboration between architect and client is that audiences as well as staff continue to appreciate the singular intimacy of this famous venue. The existing auditorium was painstakingly reconstructed to satisfy new technical requirements yet maintains the audience–performer relationship that distinguished its predecessor. Appropriately, the butcher's is the only building on the site to have survived all the changes, and it continues to serve as the shop to the street and entry to the theatrical world.

Externally, this artful collage of carefully contrived pieces acts as a riposte to the one-line architecture so common today. Nevertheless, its carefully collected 'found' components have already become a point of reference for many peers. This is clip-on architecture: a kind of theatrical Archigram, a fun palace that got built. You have the impression that the whole thing could be taken apart and put back together in another place and for other purposes.

The new Young Vic is the result of the passion for theatre of one man, Steve Tompkins (who had been coming here for three decades), delivered by a practice that does ordinary extraordinarily well, making exceptional buildings out of simple, unpretentious ideas. Its buildings never trumpet the thought and research that went into them. The concrete blocks here, for instance, far from being standard off-the-shelf items, are from specially cast moulds using slightly different mixes, giving a subtlety to the elevations that is quietly pleasing. The handrails and door handles put together raw materials in novel, eye-catching ways and are highly praised by access groups. This is architecture that is clever without being shouty. It is the opposite of skin-deep object architecture, retaining the best elements of the scheme's temporary predecessor, but adding all the things theatres need today to draw audiences out of their homes.

2008

WINNER

ACCORDIA
Cambridge
**FEILDEN CLEGG BRADLEY STUDIOS,
MACCREANOR LAVINGTON AND ALISON
BROOKS ARCHITECTS**

SHORTLIST

AMSTERDAM BIJLMER ARENA STATION
Amsterdam, The Netherlands
GRIMSHAW ARCHITECTS WITH ARCADIS

MANCHESTER CIVIL JUSTICE CENTRE
Bridge Street West, Manchester
DENTON CORKER MARSHALL

NORD PARK CABLE RAILWAY
Innsbruck, Austria
ZAHA HADID ARCHITECTS

ROYAL FESTIVAL HALL
Belvedere Road, London SE1
ALLIES AND MORRISON

WESTMINSTER ACADEMY
Harrow Road, London W2
ALLFORD HALL MONAGHAN MORRIS

JUDGES

GORDON MURRAY
Architect (chair)

DIARMUID GAVIN
Garden designer

EVA JIRICNA
Architect

KIERAN LONG
Editor of *The Architects' Journal*

SHELLEY McNAMARA
Architect

2008

ACCORDIA
Cambridge

**FEILDEN CLEGG BRADLEY STUDIOS,
MACCREANOR LAVINGTON AND ALISON
BROOKS ARCHITECTS**

On a brownfield site in Cambridge formerly owned by the
military, three very different firms of architects – Feilden
Clegg Bradley Studios, Maccreanor Lavington and Alison
Brooks Architects – have delivered some beautifully
considered homes at a density of forty-seven to the hectare
(sixty-five if you discount the generous amenity spaces) and
at a cost of just £1617 per square metre.

This is high-density housing at its very best,
demonstrating that volume housebuilders can deliver
high-quality architecture – and, as a result, improve their
own bottom line. The whole scheme is about relationships:
between architect and developer/contractor/client; and
between private and public external space, providing a new
model for outside–inside living with rooftop terraces, internal
courtyards and large semi-public community gardens.

The site straddles a broad avenue, with just one
entrance for residents permitted by the planners. In this,
the planners bowed to the wishes of the existing local
residents, for whom objection appears to be a full-time
occupation. In other matters, however, the planners, led by
the remarkable Peter Studdert, have been imaginative and
firm with objectors. It is not often that planners refuse to
grant permission unless the developers use good architects
to produce fine architecture. One might be hard-pressed
to find another authority that would allow terraces at first-
and second-floor level, instead of banning them on the

Feilden Clegg Bradley Studios'
back-to-front terraced houses,
with their characteristic chimneys,
overlook the green.

The landscaping by Andrew Grant is key to the scheme's success, and greatly impressed the Stirling judge (and landscape gardener) Diarmuid Gavin.

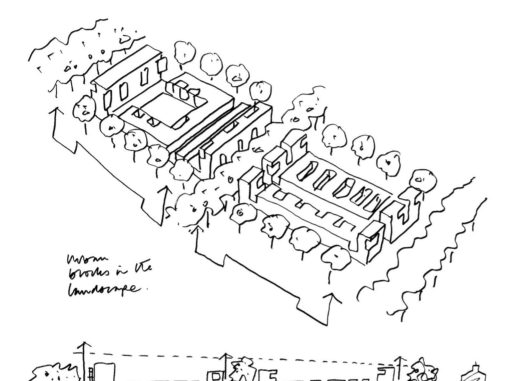

morn brooks in the landscape.

vertical edges' - horizontal interiors

A GARDEN TO:

WAKE UP TO....

RELAX IN...

SOCIALISE IN...

COOK/EAT

"GARDEN OF TERRACES"

THE SHARED GARDEN
visual amenity
productive

THE PUBLIC GARDEN
Activity & connectivity

HOUSE TERRACE 'lawn' 'summerhouse'
TERRACED HOUSE GARDEN

"A garden on many levels"

Sketches by Keith Bradley

grounds that they would overlook others. And where else would housebuilders have been dissuaded from bowing to the supposed need of homeowners for a minimum 15-metre strip of garden behind every house? Several busy residents spoke to judges about their sense of liberation from the demands of gardening. They have access to common land, where children safely play as if in some idyllic throwback to the 1950s.

Houses and flats have good-sized, well-proportioned rooms with views out ranging from the urban to rural pasture. There is plenty of variety in the house plans too, from the understated simplicity of the FCBS layouts to the highly complex plans of Maccreanor Lavington, with their two staircases and ambivalent inside–outside spaces, and the scissor-plan stairs in some of the Alison Brooks houses. The detailing, too, varies with the architect, producing a different aesthetic in each structure. These are traditional houses, but with a twist. Many elements were fabricated off-site in order to increase speed of construction, reduce waste and improve site safety and environmental performance.

This is Span-type housing for the twenty-first century, a post-Thatcherite development that is not afraid of communal

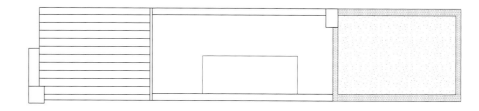

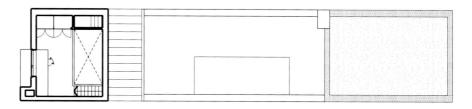

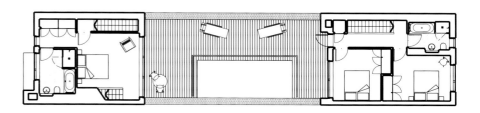

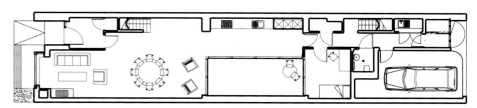

aspirations and aesthetics. There is plenty of individuality in the flexible house plans (some mews garages have been turned into studios or offices, even granny annexes) and privacy on (most of) the terraces and balconies. There are village greens and strips of common land; cars are tamed, not banned. This is architecture that treats adults as grown-ups and children as people with different needs, including stimuli for play that does not involve sitting in front of a screen or a games console, and which engenders real-life interaction with other young people.

The development proves that good modern housing sells, that a committed local authority can have a very positive influence on design, that a masterplan with a range of architects can be successful, and that the very best architecture does not need to rely on gimmicks. It is a project that will be much referenced and used as a future case study. It is architecture that gives us all hope for the future.

Talking in 2008, Keith Bradley, project director for FCBS, said: 'Landscape architect Andrew Grant was instrumental in the early moves in terms of analysing the site with its existing trees. Our whole masterplan was about this response to

Floor plans for long house (Maccreanor Lavington)

High levels of daylight are another key feature, seen here in one of the Maccreanor Lavington long houses.

Alison Brooks's bespoke semi-detached housing faces Brooklands Avenue. The two pairs of semi-detached houses form four of the forty ABA-designed houses on the site.

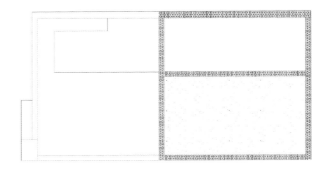

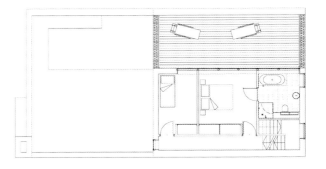

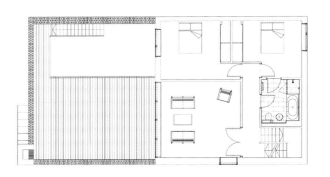

landscape. British architects used to be fantastic at designing houses, and we've lost the art somehow. There's been a lack of a patron to take on board some of those ideas.'

Alison Brooks said of Accordia: 'I think the generosity of space is just astounding. I wish it was applied to every housing development across the UK. There weren't really any limitations put on us in terms of how many square feet our flats and houses should be. So long as we provided the right number of units, we were given the freedom to produce what we thought was the best quality of space for the future purchasers.'

Richard Lavington commented: 'The advantage of having three architects designing these 400 dwellings is that there are an enormous number of different types of house. Even within the terrace we designed, there are six different types of house. And I think that richness is a really important part of why it works.'

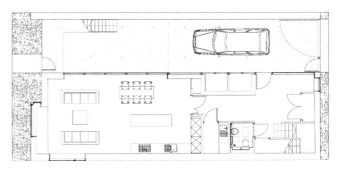

Floor plans for courtyard house (Feilden Clegg Bradley Studios)

Feilden Clegg Bradley Studios designs in higher-density mode with these apartments featuring cantilevered rooms and inset balconies.

CLIENT
Countryside Properties

STRUCTURAL ENGINEER
Richard Jackson

SERVICES ENGINEER
Roberts + Partners

LANDSCAPE ARCHITECT
Grant Associates

CONTRACTOR
Kajima Construction

CONTRACT VALUE
£38 million

IMAGES
Peter Cook – VIEW (p. 108; p. 109);
Tim Crocker (pp. 106–107; opposite;
right)

2008

AMSTERDAM BIJLMER ARENA STATION
Amsterdam, The Netherlands

GRIMSHAW ARCHITECTS WITH ARCADIS

In an Amsterdam suburb notorious for the toughness of its brutalist housing blocks – one of which was struck by a cargo jumbo jet in 1992 – Grimshaw's achievement is to have created a singular piece of urbanism. In what is a cameo of European cooperation, Grimshaw has worked with Arcadis, a Dutch multidisciplinary practice responsible for the working drawings and all the engineering. The rebuilt station, elevated 4 metres above the site of its predecessor in order to tuck a bus station under its wing, sits between the urban blocks and the vast belly of the Ajax football stadium.

Being shortlisted for the 2008 RIBA Stirling Prize was a just reward for an architect fashionably dismissed as anachronistically high tech. Grimshaw's work does revel in its engineering, but there is no harm in that. While the form-makers hide their structure behind concrete, obscured glass or ETFE, Bijlmer wears its structure on its sleeve, facing up to all its urban challenges in a mature fashion. There is something almost elephantine about the way in which the rail decks heave themselves across the plaza on heavy concrete legs, but something admirably heroic too. The steel supports also are unapologetic, the white paint emphasizing their mass.

The fact that the tracks are above ground has made a real difference at street level. To the northwest, a very broad promenade has been constructed to the Ajax stadium, and the placing of the bus station beneath the tracks establishes Bijlmer as a place of interchange. To the east, the great flat arch of the station completes the existing square. And so this complex 'edge city' intersection is given clarity by the intervention of the new station.

The architectural key to the project is the interpretation of the gaps between the tracks and the ways in which these have been transformed to make lofty and enjoyable public spaces between the ground and the platforms above. From here the dynamic can be experienced of vertical, horizontal and diagonal locomotion: the glazed lift towers versus the varying pace of trains arriving, departing and passing through, and the leisurely procession of passengers on escalators. The station, with its expressive directional structure and Oregon pine soffits to the canopies, provides the setting for this remarkable drama. Not unlike a Roman aqueduct in its transcending authority, Bijlmer Station is capable of absorbing the mistakes that all cities make and producing a good place – a fine accomplishment.

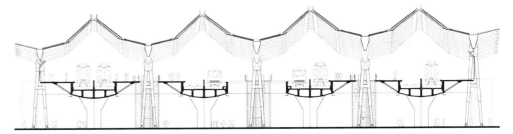

Section

Timber serves as the linking device that connects platform canopies and concourses, providing visual clarity and assisting wayfinding.

CLIENT
Prorail

STRUCTURAL/RAIL ENGINEER
Arcadis

CONTRACTOR
BESIX Nederland

CONTRACT VALUE
€130 million

IMAGES
Jan Derwig (right); Mark Humphreys (opposite)

2008

MANCHESTER CIVIL JUSTICE CENTRE
Bridge Street West, Manchester

DENTON CORKER MARSHALL

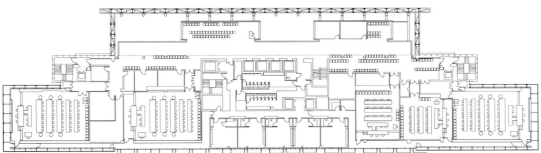

Level 11 plan

The largest court building constructed in the UK since the Royal Courts of Justice in the 1880s, Manchester Civil Justice Centre rethinks the building type. It takes the cliché about glass representing openness and makes it work on a practical level, allowing passers-by to see something of its inner workings, and permitting those who have been summonsed glimpses of the outside world from inside the courts.

Underlining the separation of civil justice from the criminal justice system, this pioneering new civic building is both open and accessible. All courts demand this separation be reflected in the plan; the same applies to making the distinction between public and private, front of house and back of house. The response here is a very literal diagram: the working courts and offices are articulated as rectilinear forms at each floor level, with the courtrooms expressed as cantilevered structures projecting from the end elevations. Meeting and waiting rooms project into the atrium. There, the lift façades, with their dull gunmetal-grey finish, and the understated trim to the boxes containing the meeting/waiting rooms – some yellow but mostly grey – give a corporate feel (in the best sense of the term) to the whole. Ironically, it seems almost like a privilege to be here.

The centre is an elegant and beautifully executed response to a complex brief, and has made a significant contribution to the regeneration of the Spinningfields area. The effective public domain is not outside but in: a glazed multi-level atrium with concourses serving all court levels. The general public can access a café in the lowest level of the atrium, overlooking the square.

The architectural expression and resolution of the environmental design set this building apart. Sustainability was integrated into the scheme from the outset. Natural ventilation to all areas and a mixed-mode ventilation system serving the courtrooms have contributed to a BREEAM rating of 'Excellent'. The external veil of grey perforated steel on the rear of the building provides solar shading and privacy for rooms of varying size behind – judges' chambers and small courts – while presenting a powerful urban image from afar and a successful piece of townscape close to.

This may be what one RIBA judge described as billboard architecture, and it is true that you would not want a city full of such buildings, but the occasional splash of highish-rise hyperbole can only help to enliven a geologically flat and mainly low-rise city.

CLIENT
Allied London

STRUCTURAL/SERVICES ENGINEER
Mott MacDonald

CONTRACTOR
Bovis Lend Lease

CONTRACT VALUE
£120 million

IMAGES
Tim Griffith (opposite; left);
Daniel Hopkinson (below)

The eleven-storey atrium forms the entrance to the biggest court building to be constructed in the UK since George Edmund Street's Royal Courts of Justice in 1882.

SHORTLISTED

NORD PARK CABLE RAILWAY
Innsbruck, Austria

ZAHA HADID ARCHITECTS

CLIENT
Nord Park Railway

STRUCTURAL ENGINEERS
Bollinger Grohmann Schneider
Ziviltechniker; Baumann + Obholzer

BRIDGE ENGINEER
ILF Beratende Ingenieure

CONTRACTOR
Strabag

CONTRACT VALUE
€6.5 million

IMAGES
Roland Halbe (below); Werner
Huthmacher (left)

Hungerburg Station, the highest point
on the cable railway. Here, passengers
have to change for the cable car to
take them to the top of the mountain.

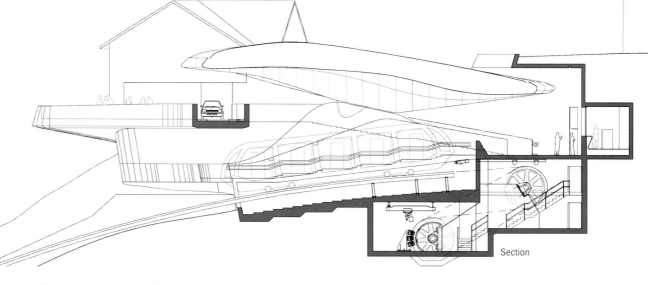

Section

A new railway line has been built to connect the mountain village of Hungerburg with the centre of Innsbruck. It offers tourists access to the high slopes, providing great views not least of Zaha Hadid's earlier ski jump, and connects villagers to the urban area 288 metres below. This was a perfect brief for Hadid: simple and precise, tying her limitless imagination to the solution of a few practical problems, while allowing its expression in a series of symbolic markers.

The line departs from close to the central square of Innsbruck and follows the course of the river, which is coloured a beautiful grey–green by glacial milk from the high mountains. A new bridge takes the train across the river, and then the railway plunges into a tunnel. In the darkness the traveller can feel the journey ratchet up into a precipitous ascent. There is one airy stop for the Alpine Zoo among steep, silent forests, then on to the main terminal in Hungerburg. The architects have worked closely with the rail engineers to produce buildings that celebrate the entire infrastructure, designing and constructing the stations at a cost of around €1 million apiece. Although all are from the same kit of parts, each is quite different, and responds in an entirely appropriate way to its context.

The architects used three interleaving systems within their design strategy. The first is a metaphorical reference to landscape: the base of each station can be read as a glacial moraine, the canopy as the glacier itself – a changeable, luminous monolith curved as if shaped by melt water. The second strategy develops the grammar cultivated by the practice through many projects. It lies somewhere between the sinuous, freely drawn line and the possibilities

presented by advanced computer software, so the form is derived from the very act of drawing. The last element, and perhaps the most telling in the development of this practice, is the engagement with the possibilities and limitations of the construction process itself.

The construction of the three-dimensionally curved glass forms is an achievement of great virtuosity. The unforgiving black lines of sealant between the glass panels help to express the structure beneath. It is hard to imagine how the necessary tolerances have been realized. In the development of Hadid's architecture from drawing to construction, this project represents a milestone in achieved form.

2008

SHORTLISTED

ROYAL FESTIVAL HALL
Belvedere Road, London SE1

ALLIES AND MORRISON

The notoriously difficult acoustics of the main concert hall have been transformed, thanks to twenty-first-century technology.

CLIENT
Royal Festival Hall, Southbank Centre

MASTERPLANNER
Rick Mather Architects

STRUCTURAL ENGINEER
Price & Myers

SERVICES ENGINEER
Max Fordham

LANDSCAPE ARCHITECT
Gross Max

CONTRACTOR
ISG Interior Exterior

CONTRACT VALUE
£110 million

IMAGES
Dennis Gilbert – VIEW

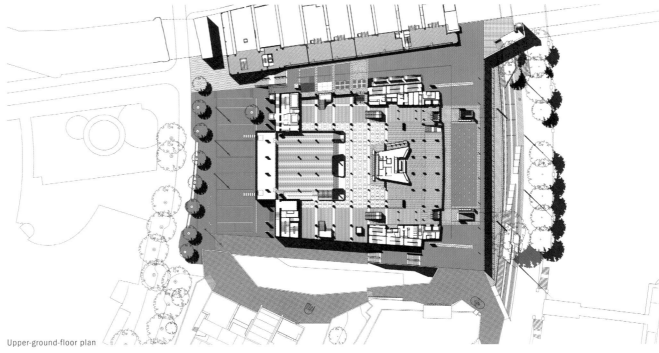

Upper-ground-floor plan

As a result of its conservation, the Royal Festival Hall has become a highly successful urban living room for London. Designed by Leslie Martin, Peter Moro and Robert Matthew for the 1951 Festival of Britain, the hall has now been restored to its original elegance and vitality. By moving offices into a linear building that hugs the adjacent railway lines, the architects have managed to get back to the essence of the Festival Hall and re-establish it as a major international venue. On the river façade, what were previously a dingy service road and an inward-looking, gloomy canteen have been transformed into a handsome parade of restaurants and shops with a much stronger relationship to the river. The outdoor terrace in front is an excellent example of successful urban space, well designed and well used. The extent of the accomplishment is demonstrated by the high turnover of the restaurants, one of which claims that its South Bank outlet is its most popular in London. Sitting with a glass of wine on this terrace must be as close as one can get to re-creating the feel of Erik Gunnar Asplund's pavilion for the Stockholm Exhibition of 1930 – or indeed the Festival of Britain itself, with its colourful, anti-utilitarian atmosphere. The public space extends not only around the building but also through it. The rationalization of the hall and its surroundings has produced a space that is now used in much the same way as Trafalgar Square: a route as well as a place to linger.

Acoustics were an imprecise art in 1951. The Royal Festival Hall was a scientific experiment, and, in the nature of experiments, the scientists did not always get it right. The acousticians of the time were pushing at the boundaries of both knowledge and materials. One of the most significant changes to the acoustics has been achieved with new baffles over the stage as well as the replacement as a lining to the hall of the cheap plywood easily available in the 1950s with solid hardwood. Two panels have been left to demonstrate how hollow and therefore reverberant the old panelling was.

This, then, is a job of great subtlety. Many things have been done so carefully and unostentatiously that one hardly notices them. The design teams at Allies and Morrison, Rick Mather Architects and landscape architect Gross Max have collaborated to give back to Londoners one of the architectural masterpieces of the twentieth century.

As in the case of most venues today, catering has become vital to underwriting the performances, with bars and restaurants outside on terraces and inside in the foyers.

2008

WESTMINSTER ACADEMY
Harrow Road, London W2

ALLFORD HALL MONAGHAN MORRIS

The Westminster Academy demonstrates how a good architect, working with an inspired head and a generous and passionately interested sponsor, can improve the educational opportunities of thousands of young people. The building, bounded by the Westway, the railway and high-rise local authority estates, provides a striking presence. In short, the project presented a physical challenge to the architects and an educational challenge to the teaching community. The academy was born out of a merger between a local junior school and what Ofsted had classified as a failing secondary school. The pupils from these pre-existing schools came from a large number of ethnic groups, and the majority did not use English as their primary language. However, this diversity and internationalism were to form the core of the academy's identity and the cultural qualities it wished to celebrate.

Overall, the organization is rational and clearly legible, with teaching and support spaces around the edges and a large, full-height court at the centre. Acoustics are managed by a series of baffles hung from the ceiling and made of cheap DIY-store doors, painted in greens and yellows on the front, white on the back. The atrium allows high levels of visibility for both staff and students. All circulation space is generous, and the study areas are defined by glass walls offering exceptionally high levels of visibility throughout. The open learning spaces are linked to facilities for eating and drinking. A 'long room' on the ground floor is designed for maximum flexibility, providing space for subdivision or open-plan activity. Most of the public spaces are characterized by bold graphics referencing aspects of the international culture that is at the heart of the school's identity. Created by Studio Myerscough, the exhortatory slogans about community can appear Maoist to adults, but they are popular with the students, who find them not in the least patronizing.

Externally, the treatment of the façade, using bands of ceramic-tile panels that shift up through shades of green to yellow, produces a building of very singular identity. The school faces directly on to the street, suggesting an intimate connection with the local community. This is architecture at the highest level, a tightly controlled tour de force. AHMM, with no previous experience of designing secondary schools, has undertaken a meticulous critical analysis of the way such public projects are being procured, taking the brief apart and responding in a pragmatic and clinically precise way.

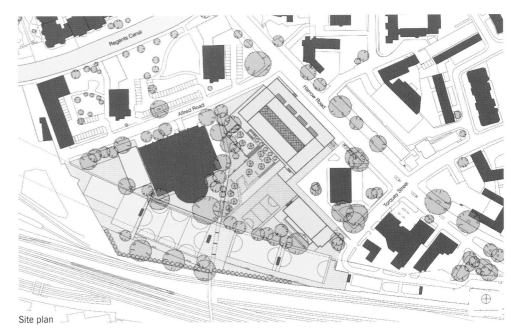

Site plan

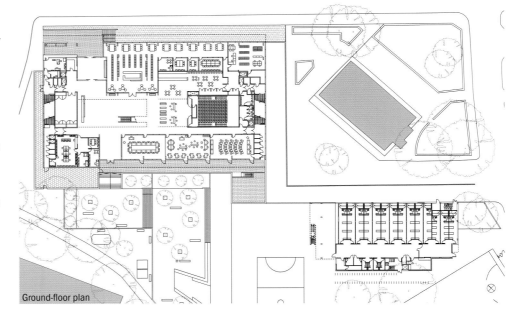

Ground-floor plan

Outside and in, this is a school that speaks the language of children and does not talk down to them.

CLIENTS
Westminster Academy; Westminster City Council; Department for Children, Schools and Families; The Exilarch's Foundation

SPONSORS
The Exilarch's Foundation; David Dangoor

LEAD CONSULTANT, STRUCTURE, SERVICES, LANDSCAPE, LIGHTING AND FF&E
Building Design Partnership

GRAPHICS
Studio Myerscough

CONTRACTOR
Galliford Try

CONTRACT VALUE
£25 million

IMAGES
Timothy Soar

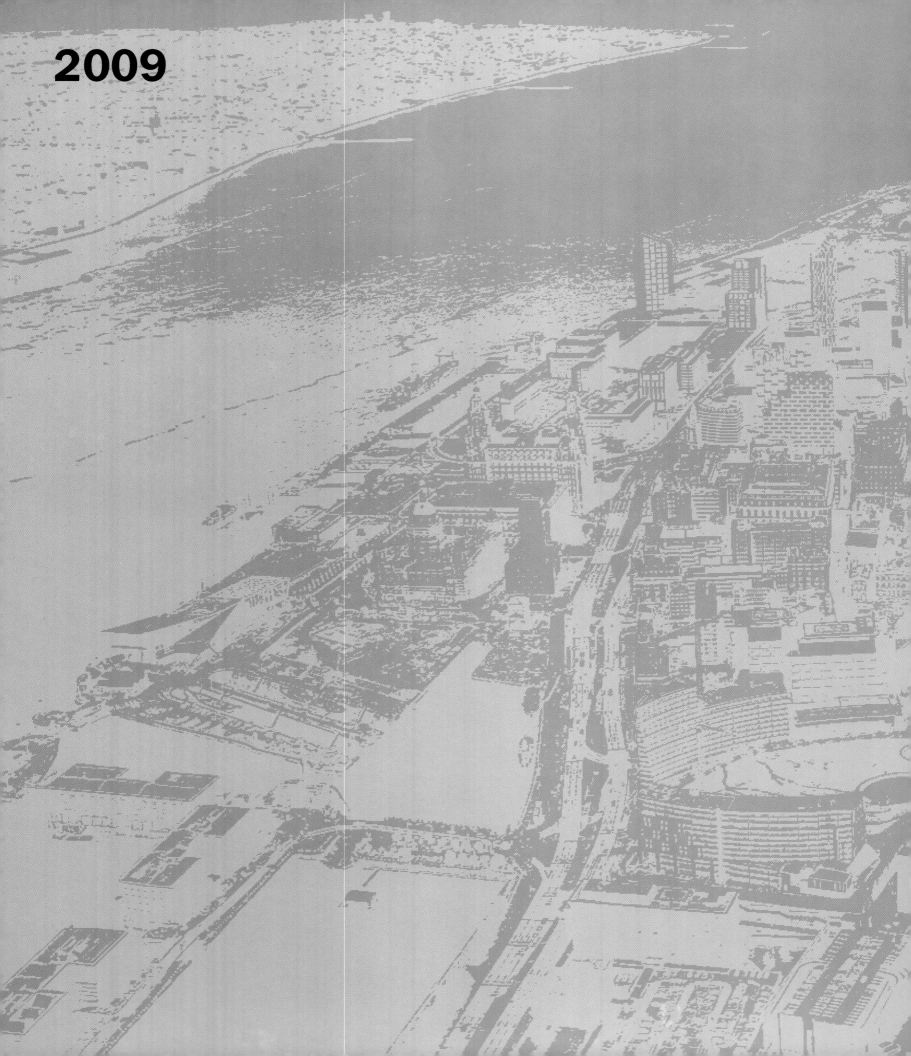

WINNER

**MAGGIE'S LONDON,
CHARING CROSS HOSPITAL**
Fulham Palace Road, London W6
ROGERS STIRK HARBOUR + PARTNERS

SHORTLIST

5 ALDERMANBURY SQUARE
London EC2
ERIC PARRY ARCHITECTS

BODEGAS PROTOS
Peñafiel, Valladolid, Spain
ROGERS STIRK HARBOUR + PARTNERS

FUGLSANG KUNSTMUSEUM
Toreby, Lolland, Denmark
TONY FRETTON ARCHITECTS

KENTISH TOWN HEALTH CENTRE
Bartholomew Road, London NW5
ALLFORD HALL MONAGHAN MORRIS

LIVERPOOL ONE MASTERPLAN
Liverpool 1
BDP (MASTERPLAN ARCHITECT)

JUDGES

JOHN TUOMEY
Architect and Stirling Prize shortlisted in 1999
and 2005 (chair)

STEPHEN BATES
Designer

THOMAS HEATHERWICK
Designer

SIR JOHN SORRELL
Designer and chair of CABE

BENEDETTA TAGLIABUE
Architect and Stirling Prize winner in 2005

2009

MAGGIE'S LONDON, CHARING CROSS HOSPITAL
Fulham Palace Road, London W6

ROGERS STIRK HARBOUR + PARTNERS

All great buildings need good clients. As a cancer-care nurse, Laura Lee (the client) promised her patient Maggie Jencks that she would carry out her dying wish: to see cancer sufferers and their families and friends offered humane facilities in which they could learn about the illness and receive support. In thirteen years since the first centre – designed by Richard Murphy and shortlisted in 1997 – opened in Edinburgh, five more, by some of the world's leading architects, including Frank Gehry and Zaha Hadid, have opened, with a further eight planned or under construction. For the latest, and the first in London, Charles Jencks turned to his old friend Richard Rogers.

The most recent in a line of Maggie's Centres designed by distinguished architects stands on a hectic corner on the Fulham Palace Road in Hammersmith. A deep-orange rendered wall puts a comforting arm around the site, making it a place apart without denying that it is a part of the city. This antithesis of a hospital provides an open house. There is no signage; everything is intuitive. There are no hinged doors except on the entrance and the toilets. As in the case of any traditional home, life is centred around the hearth – here a wood-burning stove – and the kitchen. A large table and a kettle welcome users, inviting people disturbed by news of cancer (either in themselves or in loved ones) to come in and make themselves comfortable. There are plenty of peaceful corners into which they can retreat, but mainly they congregate around this table, conversing quietly, gently getting their lives back. Rogers Stirk Harbour's serenely confident building has created a completely informal, home-like sanctuary to help patients learn to live, or die, with cancer.

The approach is via beautifully executed landscaping by Dan Pearson. The centre was conceived as a two-storey pavilion, and its positive spirit is signalled by a bold roof canopy that hovers high above the walls to sail protectively

The building plays with geometries, yet it is a warm and approachable place to visit, as befits a Maggie's Centre.

2009

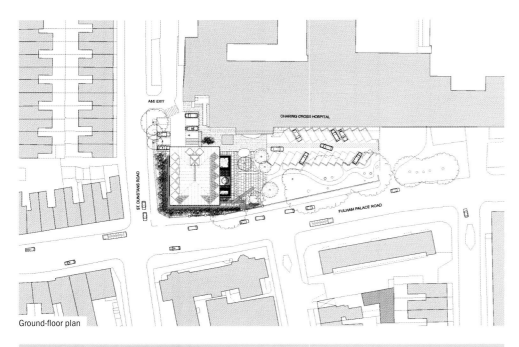

Ground-floor plan

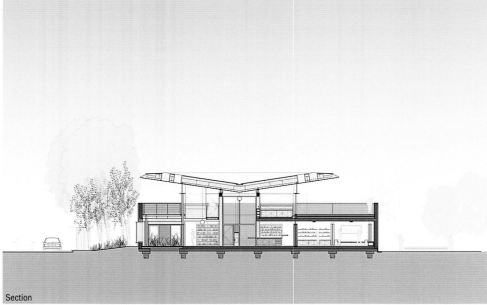

Section

over a series of intimate internal gardens, courtyards and roof terraces, also by Pearson. One large opening in the façade provides a glimpse of a courtyard garden and the table beyond; it immediately speaks of simple human pleasures, and invites us in. The building's domestic heart is washed in light and framed by concrete columns that were cast *in situ*. The concrete contractor is an artist, and it shows. Also supporting the first floor and the roof, the column arrangement is based on a 4-metre grid that provides an ideal proportion for the consultation and treatment rooms, living spaces and garden courtyards that all open off the kitchen. Privacy can be created by the use of sliding screens, translucent glass panels, or bookshelves. These are built in a light timber, as is the furniture. The client suggested IKEA; the architects persuaded Maggie's to go for something closer to Aalto.

The first floor is largely given over to administration, but it is informally arranged: staff work mainly at tables in corners, and users are free, even encouraged – by the presence of a library – to come up here. Balustrades at this level have been detailed as bookshelves and display surfaces – another example of the architects making every element of the building work in a multiplicity of modes, both beautiful and functional. This series of mezzanines, open to the floor below, feels like a tree house with views out on all four sides.

This Maggie's Centre demonstrates the power of architecture to shape our experience, and makes a fitting memorial to Maggie Keswick Jencks. Rogers Stirk Harbour has produced a timeless work of architecture that not only distils the intentions of the brief, but also expresses, in built form, compassion, sensitivity and a deep sense of our common humanity.

Speaking in 2015, the lead architect, Ivan Harbour, said of this scheme: 'Maggie's like people to think of it as

The roof canopy protects a series of tranquil internal gardens and courtyards.

a home. It's not really a home, but you might desire it as a home. It's about the way the place should feel. I always say that's the thing that separates a great building from a good building: does it feel right when you are there? Do you want to stay, or do you want to get out quickly? And, of course, with Maggie's they want you to stay.'

Richard Rogers commented in 2009: 'It's very much about repairing the spirit rather than repairing the body; somewhere you can go and shelter – that was a critical part of the brief. I have vivid memories of Maggie saying that, when you go in to see the doctor, you go in as a whole person, and you come out destroyed by the moment when he suddenly says, "You've got cancer." And what do you do; do you sit in a corridor? So this is really about taking shelter, about healing the massive wound made by that moment.'

CLIENT
Maggie's

STRUCTURAL ENGINEER
Arup

SERVICES ENGINEER
Turner & Townsend

LANDSCAPE ARCHITECT
Dan Pearson Studio

LIGHTING CONSULTANT
Speirs + Major

CONTRACTOR
Rok

CONTRACT VALUE
£2.1 million

IMAGES
Richard Bryant – Arcaid

The centre provides places for people to be as easily on their own as together – a remarkable achievement in such a small building.

2009

5 ALDERMANBURY SQUARE
London EC2

ERIC PARRY ARCHITECTS

This 35,000-square-metre office project shares the same architect–client team as Parry's previous Stirling-shortlisted building, 30 Finsbury Square (2003). When the opportunity arose to redevelop Royex House, an undistinguished 1960s office building by Richard Seifert, Scottish Widows rang Eric Parry and said, 'We've got a new challenge for you.'

It certainly was a challenge: Scottish Widows wanted to double the floor space on the same footprint, while the planners wanted to reduce the height. What's more, Parry's idea was to make the building look less massive by forming it of two staggered wings divided by a glazed belly that is cut back to admit light into the triple-height ground-floor reception space and the new square, as well as stepping it back from the ninth floor in order to counter the looming perspective that makes any tall building appear to topple towards the bystander. Both these steps reduced the available floor space. The achievement of the brief therefore represents a kind of architectural magic.

Parry believes in starting with the urban context and working his way into the building, rather than working out from the building and stitching it into a context. The important views of 5 Aldermanbury Square from the Guildhall were the first to be 'designed'. The entire structure of the building sits space-efficiently outside the floorplates. The 6-metre grid is defined by a Cor-Ten steel frame filled with reinforced concrete for fire protection. The fact that the steel frame is pre-rusted is not for aesthetic reasons – which is why Cor-Ten is usually used (here it is not visible) – but because it prevents further deterioration of the frame. This is overclad with shot-peened steel – a technique that entails blasting the surface of the steel with ceramic balls. The building is arranged in double- and, immediately above the base, triple-height bays, giving a strong sense of verticality to the elevations. Parry has created a square under and alongside his building. Adding to the sense of place are granite; board-marked concrete, its deep grain highlighted by sunshine; and a cascading rill. The previous building was ramped round with now non-compliant inclines. The architects have neatly incorporated an up-to-date ramp in the London Wall façade to link with the Barbican High Walk.

This is intelligent, considered architecture: every move is thought through, every idea tested against history and context. Here Parry has created a masterpiece amid architectural mediocrity.

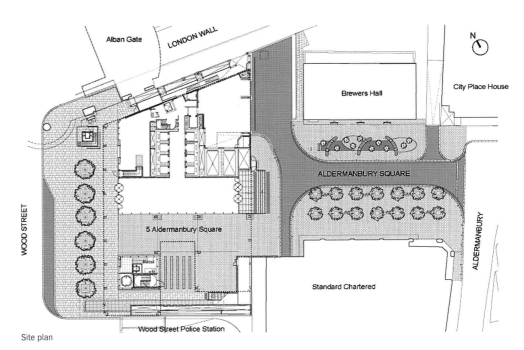

Site plan

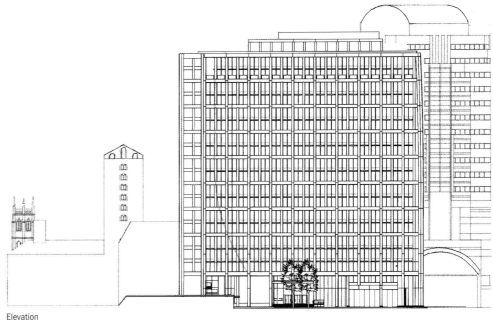

Elevation

Eric Parry's elevations are always thoughtful and materially rich, here using shot-peened steel to add texture and character.

CLIENTS
Scottish Widows with Jones Lang LaSalle

STRUCTURAL ENGINEER
Ramboll Whitbybird

SERVICES ENGINEER
Hilson Moran Partnership

CONTRACTOR
Bovis

CONTRACT VALUE
£72 million

IMAGES
Timothy Soar

SHORTLISTED

BODEGAS PROTOS
Peñafiel, Valladolid, Spain

ROGERS STIRK HARBOUR + PARTNERS

CLIENT
Bodegas Protos

EXECUTIVE ARCHITECT
Alonso Balaguer y Arquitectos
Asociados

STRUCTURAL ENGINEERS
Arup; BOMA; Agroindus

SERVICES ENGINEERS
BDSP Partnership; Grupo JG;
Agroindus

CONTRACTOR
Fomento de Construcciones y
Contratas

CONTRACT VALUE
£16 million

IMAGES
Bodegas Protos (opposite);
Katsuhisa Kida (right; below)

This is a memorable building that succeeds brilliantly in fulfilling its purpose. Many of the great names have done wineries: Herzog & de Meuron, Frank Gehry, Santiago Calatrava, even Foster + Partners (just up the road, in Gumiel de Izán). But this is no starchitect showpiece; it is a working shed that just happens also to be a landmark. The wine co-operative Bodegas Protos chose well when it selected Rogers Stirk Harbour + Partners, a firm with a not-dissimilar philosophy of co-operation leading to quality products, to give it wider international recognition. In plan, the project, led by Graham Stirk, marks a return to the thinking of the 1960s. The brief called for three separate buildings; in fact, the architects brought three functions together under one democratic roof, in the manner of Team 4's Reliance Controls building (1966) in Swindon. And what a roof it is.

In its clear, legible section, the project carries forward ideas used in the practice's Welsh Assembly building (pp. 82–83), with entry at the upper level, and the functions laid out below for all to see. Descending the spiral steel-and-glass stair to the lower level, visitors gain sudden views of the castle through the glazed gable of the arches far above them. The grapes are deposited under the end bay of the roof, and are fed by gravity into the fermentation and storage vessels at the lower level. This double-height basement uses thermal mass to provide steady environmental conditions reminiscent of the great caves that are ventilated by hobbit-house-like chimneys dotting the surrounding hillsides.

Everything was completed in sequence, so, as in the case of traditional building methods, the trades never met. First a 12-metre hole was dug, and the foundations done as a concrete box, with everything back-filled from that. The pragmatic approach required trimming 10 millimetres off the sections of structure so that they would fit on trucks, and erecting the building with virtually no scaffolding, so that it grew like a skeleton. The handsome laminated timber trusses spring from the level of the plinth, while the terracotta-tile-covered roof is a ventilated insulating cavity, floating free of the purlins by means of steel arms.

The plinth itself is of a raw-finish, top-sliced local stone, usually broken up for aggregate; the smoother stuff is used for internal walls and those of the elliptical sunken courtyard. This space takes its form (as well as its material) from the castle, of which there is another perfectly framed view.

The roof is as well composed as any façade, responding to the view from the castle. Terracotta tiles take their cue from the arches, and complement surrounding buildings.

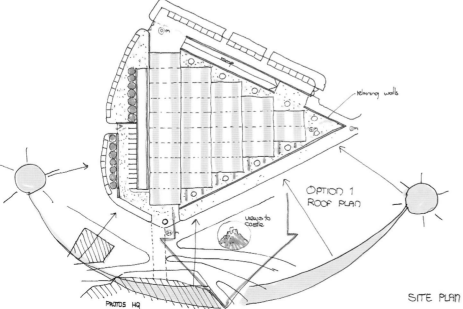

OPTION 1
ROOF PLAN

retaining walls

views to castle

PROTOS HQ

SITE PLAN

2009

FUGLSANG KUNSTMUSEUM
Toreby, Lolland, Denmark

TONY FRETTON ARCHITECTS

CLIENT
Bygningsfonden

EXECUTIVE ARCHITECT
BBP Arkitekter

STRUCTURAL/SERVICES ENGINEER
Alectia (formerly Birch & Krogboe)

LANDSCAPE ARCHITECT
Schønherr Landskab

CONTRACTOR
C.C. Brun Enterprise

CONTRACT VALUE
£6.5 million

IMAGES
Hélène Binet

The new building responds to the forms and materials of the nearby farm buildings.

This project, like so much of Tony Fretton's work, concerns the sublime in the context of the ordinary and everyday. The art gallery is part of a long-term programme in Denmark to relocate cultural facilities to rural areas in order to encourage greater exposure and understanding of art beyond its usual urban audience; given the gallery's pre-eminent national collection of landscape paintings (1720–1970), it is an appropriate move. Client Anna Højer Petersen's brief called for an approachable, domestic-scale gallery that nonetheless has presence. It also stipulated that the building should be a place where one can spend time with the art. Fretton's response was partially to enclose small pockets off the main long gallery (really a broad corridor), just big enough for a couple of people to look at one or two pieces of art. But Fretton disregarded one key element of the brief. It called for

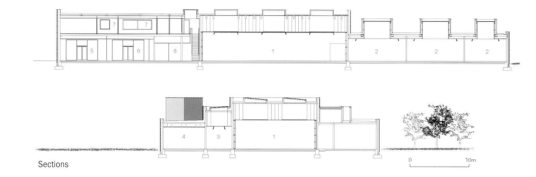

Sections

A room at the end of the plan, where a view of nature is allowed to compete with the art on display.

the open-ended courtyard to be closed off by the museum. Instead, he turned his gallery through 90 degrees, leaving clear views across meadowland to the sea.

The building is modest: low, clad in brick, with small, warm, homely galleries inside, and entered through a 'kitchen-café' and bookshop. There is more than a commercial imperative at work here. The arrangement is also domestic and non-threatening to an audience generally unused to high art. The architects wanted each room to have a different character, aiming for juxtaposition and yet familiarity. Fretton believes that the architecture should never dominate the art; that it should encourage one to look at the paintings, but that at the periphery one should be invigorated. The galleries are top-lit and arranged in a circle in order to encourage meandering; their expressiveness is restrained to

the extent that windows are almost entirely absent, so that the visitor's concentration focuses on the art, except for two rooms at the far end, which draw one through the building. After studying landscape art on the journey, the visitor is then presented with the real thing, framed by architecture.

Fretton describes his architecture as rear-garde rather than avant-garde; he is not afraid to be old-fashioned if that is what is appropriate. Like his Lisson Gallery in London, Fuglsang resembles found space. It is clearly an erudite project, with nods in its composition to architectural history. It feels almost as if it could have been built in any decade since the 1920s. That is quite a compliment.

2009

KENTISH TOWN HEALTH CENTRE
Bartholomew Road, London NW5

ALLFORD HALL MONAGHAN MORRIS

Site plan

CLIENT
Camden & Islington Community
Solutions

STRUCTURAL ENGINEER
Elliott Wood

SERVICES ENGINEER
Peter Deer and Associates

GRAPHICS
Studio Myerscough

CONTRACTOR
Morgan Ashurst

CONTRACT VALUE
£10.1 million

IMAGES
Rob Parrish (opposite, top); Timothy
Soar (right; opposite, bottom)

Kentish Town Health Centre sets a new standard for the National Health Service. The client, Dr Roy Macgregor, championed a project that represents a fusion of health practice, architecture and art, resulting in a building that is uplifting for both staff and patients. Architecturally and medically, this is a Finsbury Health Centre for the twenty-first century.

Composed both internally and externally of crisp-white rendered walls punctured by black-framed windows, the architecture derives its strength from the many visual cross-connections created by its internal and external voids, which the architects compare to a game of Jenga. Consulting rooms and stairs enjoy views into the triple-height central street and waiting area around which the plan is organized, and this principle is extended to smaller light wells on secondary circulation routes, which give access to small balconies. The brief asked for lots of daylight and for outdoor spaces directly accessible from the consulting rooms (these have helped with staff recruitment and retention). It also required the vast majority of the mature trees on the site to be retained.

The rhythm of the façades is broken up horizontally by square windows for the surgeries and linear windows for the open-plan areas, and vertically by the cantilevers, which are themselves responses to the surrounding trees, an effort to avoid root damage. The building is about as green as a health centre can be: the stack effect is used in the open-plan areas, with rooflights opening automatically for night-time cooling and solar wind-catchers drawing air through the cellular rooms. The only mechanical ventilation is in some internal rooms, where it is essential to prevent the spread of infections.

The signage is trademark AHMM. Studio Myerscough, originally briefed to create a letterhead, ended up doing everything from the large exterior graphic panel marking the entrance to the pictograms that guide people round the building. There is neither a conventional sign nor scarcely an NHS blue-and-white logo in sight, although the client asked for one just to ensure that people realize this highly specced building really is part of our under-appreciated NHS (despite it being maintained by the private sector).

The project is exemplary in its approach to sustainability and, in addition to natural ventilation, includes the use of recycled materials. Why can't all health clinics be like this?

SHORTLISTED

LIVERPOOL ONE MASTERPLAN
Liverpool 1

BDP (MASTERPLAN ARCHITECT)

KEY

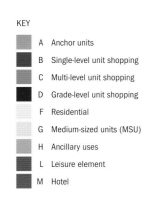

	A	Anchor units
	B	Single-level unit shopping
	C	Multi-level unit shopping
	D	Grade-level unit shopping
	F	Residential
	G	Medium-sized units (MSU)
	H	Ancillary uses
	L	Leisure element
	M	Hotel

ARCHITECTS
Aedas; Allies and Morrison;
Austin-Smith:Lord; BDP; Brock
Carmichael Architects; Craig Foster
Architects; CZWG; Dixon Jones;
FAT; Glenn Howells Architects;
Greig & Stephenson; Gross Max;
Groupe-Six; Hawkins\Brown;
Haworth Tompkins; John McAslan
+ Partners; Leach Rhodes Walker;
Marks Barfield Architects; Owen Ellis
Architects; Page\Park; Pelli Clarke
Pelli Architects; Roberts Limbrick;
Squire and Partners; Stephenson Bell
Architects; Studio Three; Wilkinson
Eyre Architects

CLIENT
Grosvenor

STRUCTURAL ENGINEER
Waterman Partnership

SERVICES ENGINEER
WSP

CONTRACTORS
Laing O'Rourke; Balfour Beatty

CONTRACT VALUE
£500 million

IMAGES
Grosvenor (right); Paul McMullin
(opposite, top); David Millington
(opposite, bottom)

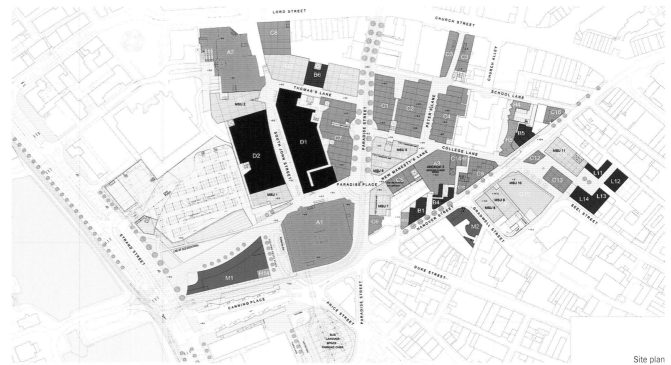

Site plan

The Liverpool One Masterplan has single-handedly reversed
the fortunes of the city by bringing a new social and economic
vibrancy to these previously derelict 17 hectares at its
heart – the result of Second World War bomb damage and
subsequent poor-quality redevelopment. The near-billion-
pound project is recognized as one of the most significant
city-regeneration schemes in Europe.

Rod Holmes, aided and succeeded by Guy Butler, has
led Grosvenor's drive for quality and guided all aspects of
the design and construction process. To engage three major
architects might be deemed brave; to employ twenty-six is
sheer but brilliantly successful madness.

The greatest danger was to create monoculture. Instead,
egged on by BDP, Grosvenor took the radical decision to base
the plan of its new shopping centre not on the mall but on
the original grain of the old city streets. So the scheme looks
as if it has developed over at least twenty-five years rather
than the mere ten it has actually taken. Another advantage
of this apparently piecemeal approach is that parts of it
can be replaced when they have reached the end of their
natural lives, rather than the whole thing needing to be
comprehensively redeveloped.

Masterplanning must draw a fine line between being
prescriptive and being permissive. Bizarrely perhaps, there
are five 'quarters' to this scheme, each with a subtly different
character. The masterplan allows for exceptions to its few
rules, and lets individual buildings stand out and draw
attention to themselves. As a consequence, the area still feels
like Liverpool. At the heart of the plan, Allies and Morrison
has created a building – more of an articulated urban block
– clad in prefabricated panels of a German limestone with a
hammered finish. It gives a sense of permanence – of history
even – and will no doubt come to be thought of as being as
important as the nearby trio of grand buildings (Royal Liver
Building, Cunard Building and Port of Liverpool Building)
overlooking the Mersey. This, far more than the new Museum
of Liverpool, is the city's Fourth Grace. Almost as impressive
are Dixon Jones's elegant covered arcade in bronze, which
plays tricks with perspective, and Haworth Tompkins's
housing, which is every bit as characterful as its scheme
on the South Bank in London. The overall result is a vibrant
and economically successful retail, leisure and mixed-use
quarter – an entirely revitalized city centre that now provides
a major urban connection to the Liverpool Docks.

2010

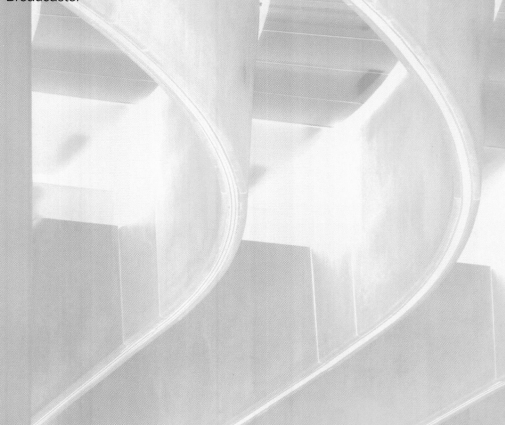

WINNER

MAXXI
Museo Nazionale delle Arti del XXI Secolo
Rome, Italy
ZAHA HADID ARCHITECTS

SHORTLIST

**ASHMOLEAN MUSEUM OF ART
AND ARCHAEOLOGY**
Beaumont Street, Oxford
RICK MATHER ARCHITECTS

BATEMAN'S ROW
London EC2
THEIS + KHAN ARCHITECTS

CHRIST'S COLLEGE
Guildford, Surrey
DSDHA

CLAPHAM MANOR PRIMARY SCHOOL
Belmont Road, London SW4
dRMM

NEUES MUSEUM
Berlin, Germany
DAVID CHIPPERFIELD ARCHITECTS

JUDGES

RUTH REED
RIBA President (chair)

IVAN HARBOUR
Architect, Stirling Prize winner in 2006 and
2009, and shortlisted in 1997, 2000, 2002,
2006 and 2009

LISA JARDINE, CBE
Historian and writer

EDWARD JONES
Architect and Stirling Prize shortlisted in 2001
and 2009

MARK LAWSON
Broadcaster

2010

MAXXI
Museo Nazionale delle Arti del XXI Secolo
Rome, Italy

ZAHA HADID ARCHITECTS

The museum does not feel like Rome, but is all the more exciting for that, juxtaposed with local army barracks and industrial warehouses, but with glimpses of distant views to Roman rooftops and cupolas. Its suburban context allows it a freedom denied to architects in the centre of Rome (in recent times only Richard Meier has got away with modernism in the Eternal City).

The original competition-winning entry of 1999 proposed removing many – but not all – of the military buildings on the site. By distorting the existing suburban grid, the architects have introduced a field of elements that suggest a very untraditional museum. The result is a building of paths and routes, a museum where the curators have to be inventive in their hanging and placement of twenty-first-century artworks that have been collected since the inception of the project – and the century. The permeable plaza re-creates routes and connections, but also forces you to consider the

new context that is created to engage with the activities within. The whole is behind a 2.5-metre-high industrial aluminium mesh fence, which safeguards the outdoor art. The setting has echoes of OMA's Casa da Música (pp. 94–95), an impression reinforced by the perched box of an upper gallery with a panoramic window, reached by an array of stairs, ramps and lifts. As Rem Koolhaas has done in Porto, here in Rome Hadid has created an object in the city that challenges but intrigues; one that, far from alienating visitors, tempts them inside.

Despite the drama of its exterior forms, internally the museum is rationally organized into five main suites. The whole is bravely daylit with a sinuous roof of controllable skylights, louvres and beams, while conforming to the very strict climate-control requirements of modern galleries; the skylights both orientate and excite the visitor, and also produce uplifting spaces. One mansion facing the main

Maxxi's form derives not from the rectilinear lines of the city, but from the organic line of the adjacent River Tiber.

2010

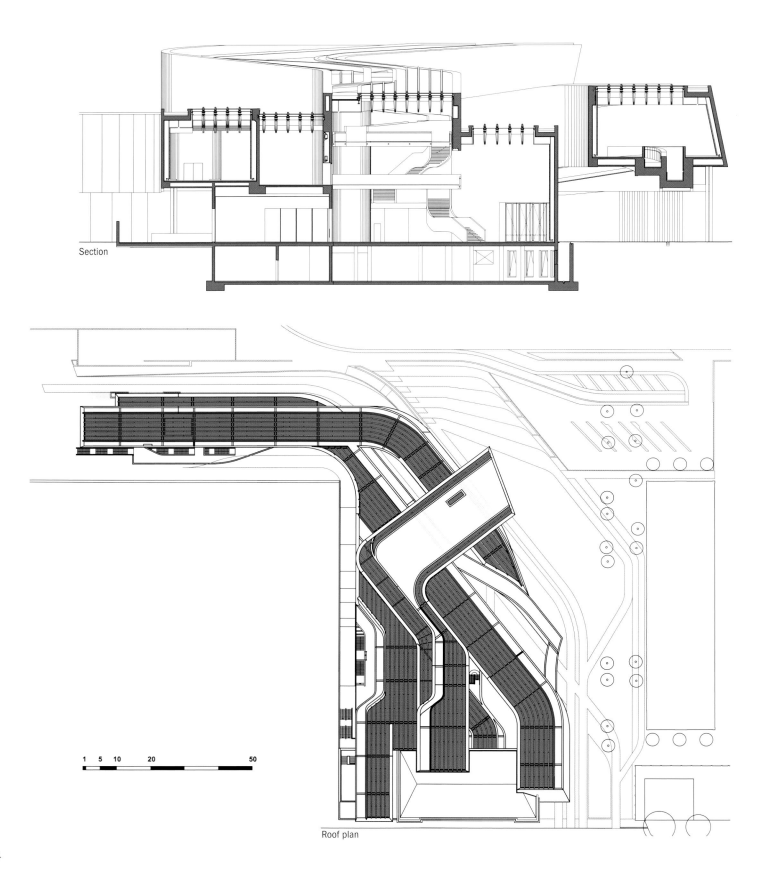

Section

1 5 10   20   50

Roof plan

The sinuous forms of Zaha Hadid's architecture abound inside the museum as well as externally.

street has been retained: the new building clutches it in the same way a bird clutches something in its beak. Inside, the old building reveals its structure as four cast-iron columns supporting the roof. The architects were not required, but rather chose to retain this and the warehouse buildings (also with orthogonal geometry); these spaces are used for the storage of artworks. Together, they make a quiet contrast with the structural pyrotechnics of the new design, and enrich the whole composition.

MAXXI is described as a building for the staging of art and, while provocative at many levels, it shows a maturity and calmness that belie the complexities of its form and organization. The nature of the project meant that everything had to be overspecified; throughout the design process the architects had no idea what would be hung in this series of rooms, so walls that are able to bear a tonne of rusting steel might be graced by miniatures. In use, in addition to

the innovative hanging, video projections bounce off the white curves, animating the spaces. This is great interior architecture, with form and function smoothly integrated in the way they were at Hadid's BMW factory in Leipzig (shortlisted in 2005).

MAXXI is a mature piece of architecture, the distillation of years of experimental projects, only a fraction of which ever got built. It is the quintessence of Hadid's constant attempt to create a landscape, a series of cavernous spaces drawn with a free, roving line. Rather than prescribing routes, the resulting piece gives the visitor a sense of exploration, as befits an art gallery (though less a museum with its own narrative).

When she won the Royal Gold Medal in 2016, Zaha Hadid said of MAXXI: 'Rome is a very important project that took a long time to do, and I enjoyed doing it. In a way, it's not the same, but it has similar qualities to the unbuilt

2010

The scale of Hadid's cavernous spaces dwarfs their users, rendering them as players in a drama.

CLIENTS
Ministero per i Beni e le Attività
Culturali; Fondazione MAXXI; Ministero
delle Infrastrutture e dei Trasporti

STRUCTURAL ENGINEERS
Studio SPC; SKM Anthony Hunt;
The OK Design Group

SERVICES ENGINEERS
Max Fordham; The OK Design Group

CONTRACTORS
Consortium MAXXI 2006; Italiana
Costruzioni; Società Appalti
Costruzioni

CONTRACT VALUE
€150 million

IMAGES
Iwan Baan (p. 143 top; p. 145;
opposite; left; below); Roland Halbe
(pp. 142–43)

Peak in Hong Kong. It has also many ideas I've thought about for a long time and which culminate in this building, and so I'm very happy that it won the Stirling. The idea is of being in a museum that is almost a landscape in which you are wandering around, as if in a hill town. That was not deliberate, but that is what it feels like. And what is also engaging about MAXXI is that it's very rigorous as a design, but it's also very contextual in an interesting way, because all the geometries match existing geometries on the site. I think you can create in an art gallery multiple experiences. You don't have to dictate what the person has to look at and the way in which they look at it; your mind can adjust to more than one piece of information, so this multiplied experience can be very intriguing.'

2010

ASHMOLEAN MUSEUM OF ART AND ARCHAEOLOGY
Beaumont Street, Oxford

RICK MATHER ARCHITECTS

KEY
1 Exploring the Past
2 Human Image
3 Conservation Gallery
4 Conservation Gallery
5 Textiles
6 Reading and Writing
7 Money
8 Art to Ashmolean

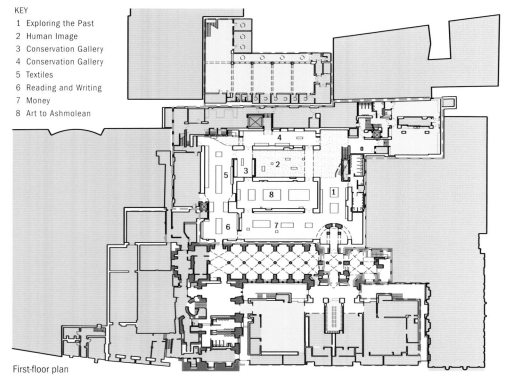

First-floor plan

The bar for this project could not have been set higher: in order to double the display space of the oldest museum in Britain while retaining Charles Cockerell's Grade I-listed building of 1845, the architect was effectively required to put a ship in a bottle. The resulting building – 9000 square metres of new accommodation that remains largely invisible to the public realm, built via a single narrow access off St Giles' only a couple of metres wide – clears that bar by a mile to give a world-class institution a worthy new home. It has virtually no external walls, but seven different party walls. Yet this is by no means 'mere' interior architecture. Rather, it is the culmination of a working life spent by the architect in refining the detailing of galleries, houses and restaurants to create a deeply satisfying series of interlocking spaces.

As one enters through the Cockerell façade, the eye is drawn to a daylit space beyond. This central atrium, modest in plan yet dramatic in section, rises through six floors and provides an excellent quality of illumination, even on the lower ground floor, while avoiding light levels that could damage exhibits. The pellucid light that washes through the atrium, bathing the polished plaster walls, has an almost surreal quality. A subtly curved staircase cascades down one wall, stepping outwards as it descends to produce a three-dimensional form of originality and great effect, as if it were in an Escher drawing. Its raked solid balustrades are set at a different angle from the glazed balustrading, giving an orange-peel effect that adds to the beguiling composition.

The route through the museum navigates cleverly interleaved and interconnected double- and single-height spaces in a rich spatial journey. Complementing the clarity and ingenuity of the architecture, the design team at Metaphor under Stephen Greenberg (himself an architect) has brilliantly curated the displays and graphics on the theme of 'Crossing Cultures, Crossing Time'. This theme is reflected in the architecture, with carefully controlled (though seemingly random) visual relationships between items in the collection.

Dr Christopher Brown, director of the museum, asserted: 'This is Rick Mather's finest building to date, and I have no doubt it'll be recognized very soon as one of the outstanding museum buildings of the twenty-first century.' He is right; this is indeed a world-class building.

Opposite: Only the sliver of the restaurant, peeking above the parapet of Charles Cockerell's classicism, gives any hint of Rick Mather's modernist masterpiece within.

Left and below: Photograph as section, staircase as exhibit: the architecture is as rich as the museum's contents.

CLIENTS
University of Oxford; Ashmolean Museum of Art and Archaeology

STRUCTURAL ENGINEER
Dewhurst MacFarlane & Partners

SERVICES ENGINEER
Atelier Ten

EXHIBITION DESIGN
Metaphor

CONTRACTOR
BAM Construct UK

CONTRACT VALUE
£62 million

IMAGES
Richard Bryant – Arcaid (above);
Andy Matthews – Rick Mather
Architects (opposite; left; left, top)

2010

BATEMAN'S ROW
London EC2

THEIS + KHAN ARCHITECTS

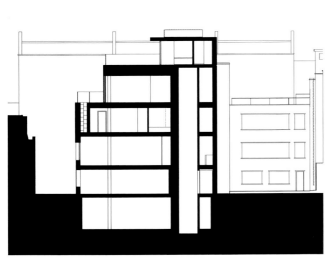

Section

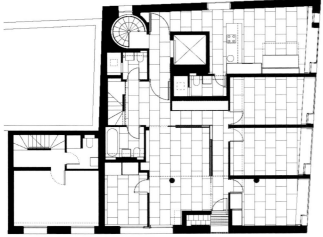

Second-floor plan

Open-plan living in London rarely comes as good as this: exposed concrete, great views, terraces overlooking London, all wrapped up in a warm brick package.

CLIENTS
Soraya Khan; Patrick Theis

STRUCTURAL ENGINEER
F.J. Samuely and Partners

CONTRACTOR
Silver Interiors Design & Build

CONTRACT VALUE
£1.6 million

IMAGES
Nick Kane – Arcaid

This is a clever development by an architect–client couple for a mix of uses, including their home and office. It is on five floors over a basement, and completely fills its corner site. The mix includes four dwellings (an apartment on three floors, plus one studio flat and two larger flats), the architects' own office on the first floor and an art gallery on the ground floor and basement. In section, the scheme skilfully adjusts the floor heights, creating taller spaces for the gallery, the studio and the principal living space.

A base of dark brick defines the back-of-pavement of the narrow streets, but the building becomes progressively lighter towards the top, with an American quality to the living room and terraces on the top floors, which provide incredible views of the City of London. The scheme even has its own High Line – although, unlike in New York, it is still a working London Overground line, with trains sliding past at fourth-floor level.

The principal apartment is accessed via a dual-entry lift, which connects directly into the living space, as well as by a castle-like spiral stair. The office, the gallery and the flats have separate stairs and entrances from the street, but are connected by the same lift.

In its response to its surroundings, its scale and its mix of uses, this development defines a vision for the future of the Shoreditch neighbourhood. It provides an environment for family living within a tough urban context and an apartment with qualities that could not easily be found in a house. It has a fortress-like quality, towering over the hubbub of the surrounding area on weekend evenings, providing a safe haven and respite for the couple and their children.

At no point during the lengthy process of realizing the project – ten years from initial, protracted negotiations with adjoining owners and the raising of funds for construction – was there a loss of ambition. The home created is a great achievement.

The architects have found a way of developing a tight, difficult site in a way that is both spatially and aesthetically rich. This is a relevant piece of city-making that is ordinary in its programme, yet executed with extraordinary care and judgement, taking it into the realms of the special. London and the post-Crash housing market require far more of its kind.

SHORTLISTED

CHRIST'S COLLEGE
Guildford, Surrey

DSDHA

CLIENTS
Diocese of Guildford; Surrey County
Council

STRUCTURAL ENGINEER
Adams Kara Taylor

SERVICES ENGINEER
Atelier Ten

CONTRACTOR
Wates Construction

CONTRACT VALUE
£14.4 million

IMAGES
Hélène Binet (right; opposite,
bottom); DSDHA (opposite, top)

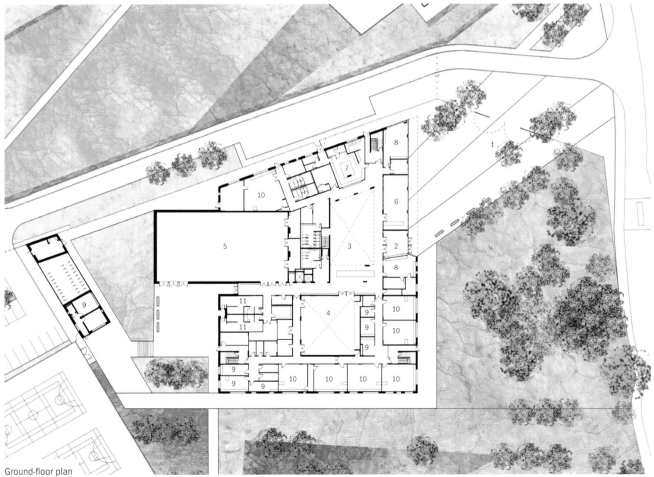

KEY
1 Main entrance
2 Reception
3 Atrium
4 Theatre
5 Sports hall
6 Library
7 Kitchen
8 Staff
9 Group teaching spaces
10 Classrooms
11 Changing rooms

Ground-floor plan

Constructed of predominantly dark materials, this is a sophisticated school, letting in top light, particularly in the atrium, and with breakout terraces at first-floor level.

This clever design for a secondary school is a worthy companion to the adjoining special-needs school by the same practice, winner of an RIBA Award in 2009. But whereas that was a single storey, as befits a building for young people with many learning and physical difficulties, this new school achieves a great deal on three compact levels, yet has a gratifying generosity of circulation and inner courtyard spaces.

The five faculties within the school are boldly identified with brightly coloured doors in a predominantly grey, black and concrete series of internal finishes that are subtle, grown-up and calming. The central atrium has to perform many flexible functions. Its walls and ceiling are lined in cheap pine boards, yet because of the quality of the design the space is not sauna-like. Although it is an internal space, it is illuminated evenly by large rooflights. The tables at one edge of the space accommodate computers for informal teaching; other dining tables can be swept away to allow trampolining or other games – although there is a splendid, robust, daylit gym in another part of the college. The atrium is, however, primarily a meeting place, the true heart of a fine building where the architect seems to have thought of everything. It is a mature piece that will help its pupils to develop into well-rounded adults.

The building has an innovative natural ventilation system that works well on the hottest of summer days and is subtly manifested on the deep-brown brickwork of the external walls as occasional patterns of gaps in the pointing. The fenestration is equally handsomely arranged in each façade, has deep reveals, and in places accentuates key views across Guildford. One tall window, which illuminates a stairwell, contains one of the biggest single pieces of glass obtainable in the United Kingdom. Although the school cost less than £2000 per square metre, such details demonstrate that nowhere have corners noticeably been cut. The classrooms are sturdy, functional and adaptable spaces. Staff and students are clearly delighted with their building, which is one that will stand the test of time.

DSDHA has been both inspired by its Swiss teaching experience and informed by its understanding of the needs of British schoolchildren, who were so woefully served by politicians and many architects in the latter part of the twentieth century. It would be tragic if the efforts of the practice are stymied by the current economic climate and our response to it.

2010

CLAPHAM MANOR PRIMARY SCHOOL
Belmont Road, London SW4

dRMM

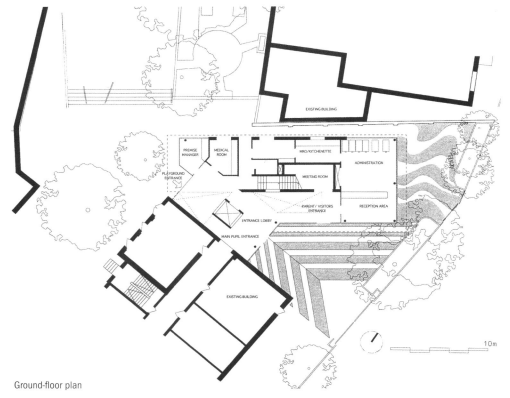

Ground-floor plan

This jewel-like project is a free-standing addition to a nineteenth-century London Board school. In the words of the architects, it 'plugs into' the existing building, allowing the school to work as a single entity. The multicoloured glass cladding is the first thing that catches the viewer's eye, but this is no straightforward glass box. The panels, although all glazed externally, are internally variously transparent, translucent and opaque. As well as greatly enhancing the energy performance of the building, this arrangement allows teachers to attach work to the coloured pinboard lining panels. It also affords a degree of privacy.

The building forms a simple rectangle in the gap between two existing buildings, and its diagonal relation to the existing school has created space for a transparent atrium that separates old and new. There is an exciting tension here that reinforces the conceptual idea and the sense of movement through the shared circulation space. For reasons of security, there are separate entrances for children and visitors, both leading off the small playground. The new form makes some interesting external spaces that have been triumphantly exploited by the architects as pocket gardens; the angled geometry also provides a very successful and secure entry sequence, with a visitors' holding point, a highly visible school office and a reception.

The 'newness' and modernity of the proposal give the project a non-institutional lightness of touch, and there are hints of post-war prefabricated building systems and an unashamed conviction in technology. The façade system allows good light and views at different heights for children and adults, and the use of coloured panels, in what one commentator has called 'boisterous polychromy', provides the scheme with a singular identity. Internally, there are no corridors; one accesses the classrooms either through the adjoining spaces or from the central gallery leading off the main lift and stairwell. All internal spaces are finished to a very high standard, with perforated acoustic panelling throughout (timber for the walls and fibreboard for the ceilings) acting as a unifying surface. Overall, the project is an inventive and uplifting example of what the next generation of school buildings could be. It avoids generic solutions, and uses the best contemporary thinking about what makes a good educational environment. It is also clearly the result of a positive collaboration between the architects, their teams and a strong headmaster with a clear educational vision.

Colour is key to this Clapham primary school, particularly in the glazed panels, some of which read through, while others are obscured but still use the same palette.

CLIENT
Lambeth AMPD

STRUCTURAL ENGINEER
Michael Hadi Associates

SERVICES ENGINEER
Fulcrum Consulting

CONTRACTOR
The Construction Partnership

CONTRACT VALUE
£2.5 million

IMAGES
Jonas Lencer

2010

NEUES MUSEUM
Berlin, Germany

DAVID CHIPPERFIELD ARCHITECTS

CLIENT
Stiftung Preussischer Kulturbesitz

RESTORATION ARCHITECT
Julian Harrap Architects

STRUCTURAL ENGINEER
Ingenieurgruppe Bauen

SERVICES ENGINEER
Jaeger, Mornhinweg + Partner

CONTRACTOR
Bundesamt für Bauwesen und
Raumordnung

CONTRACT VALUE
€200 million

IMAGES
Candida Hoefer – VG Bild-Kunst,
Bonn 2009 (opposite, top); SMB/
Ute Zscharnt for David Chipperfield
Architects (opposite, bottom); Ute
Zscharnt (below)

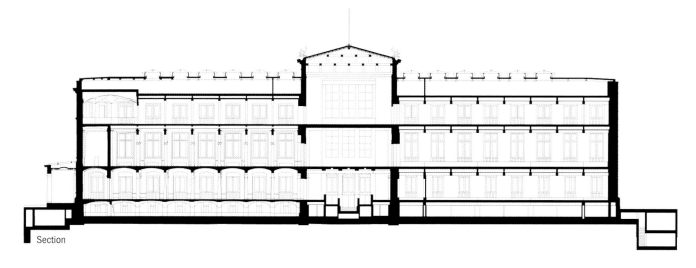

Section

The Neues Museum, on Museum Island, was designed by Friedrich August Stüler, a pupil of Karl Friedrich Schinkel, and built between 1841 and 1859 to show off the archaeological and scientific prowess of one of Europe's leading powers. In a way, it was Prussia's answer to Britain's Great Exhibition of 1851. The museum houses Egyptian and prehistoric/early archaeological collections, and is a centre for active scientific research and public dissemination. A uniquely close collaboration between the client, the Chipperfield practice and that most meticulous of conservation architects, Julian Harrap, has resulted in an exceptionally coherent and holistic piece of architecture.

The key architectural aim was to reinstate the original volumes and repair the parts remaining after the Second World War. The original sequence of rooms was restored by the new spaces, thereby creating continuity with the existing structure. The archaeological restoration philosophy follows the guidelines in the Charter of Venice (1964) respecting the historic structure in its different states of 'as found' preservation. The original structure and decoration are emphasized in terms of spatial context and materiality, but repairs and restoration respond in a clearly articulated yet sensitive manner. This is no pastiche. The same archaeological approach has been extended to the elevations of the building: the rebuilt wing and one corner are done in plain, randomly coloured and laid recycled bricks, with windows mirroring, though not slavishly copying, the originals. The insertion and integration of a

Opposite: Until recently a bombed-out, badly repaired shell, the Neues Museum has been transformed into the greatest showpiece of Berlin's Museum Island.

Below: The grand staircase is one of two big-gesture insertions (the other being the free-standing structure in one inner court that adds floor space); elsewhere, the scheme is characterized by its tact and restraint.

new interior architecture and museum environment have been impeccably judged, the cool modernism a perfect foil to both the exuberant invention of Stüler and the ancient objects on display. The new spaces are tranquil but far from neutral. From the austerity of the Central Staircase Hall to the soaring, light-filled Egyptian Courtyard, a great variety of spatial experience has been achieved while maintaining a coherent architectural expression through a controlled palette of materials and detailing. Precast concrete is the principal structural medium, and the overall result is one of consistency, quality and understated beauty. Nothing is left to chance; there are no forgotten or unloved corners. This is a museum of architectural history as much as one of archaeology. The museum directorate laudably resisted the temptation to present the visitor with too many exhibits. Less is indeed more in both the architecture and the display; there are lessons here for other museums and galleries.

2011

WINNER

EVELYN GRACE ACADEMY
Shakespeare Road, London SE24
ZAHA HADID ARCHITECTS

SHORTLIST

AN GAELÁRAS
Great James Street, Derry
O'DONNELL + TUOMEY

THE ANGEL BUILDING
St John Street, London EC1
ALLFORD HALL MONAGHAN MORRIS

MUSEUM FOLKWANG
Essen, Germany
DAVID CHIPPERFIELD ARCHITECTS

ROYAL SHAKESPEARE AND SWAN THEATRES
Stratford-upon-Avon, Warwickshire
BENNETTS ASSOCIATES

THE VELODROME
Queen Elizabeth Olympic Park, London E20
HOPKINS ARCHITECTS

JUDGES

ANGELA BRADY
RIBA President (chair)

ALISON BROOKS
Architect and Stirling Prize winner in 2008

SIR PETER COOK
Architect and Stirling Prize shortlisted in 2004

HANIF KARA
Structural engineer

DAN PEARSON
Landscape designer

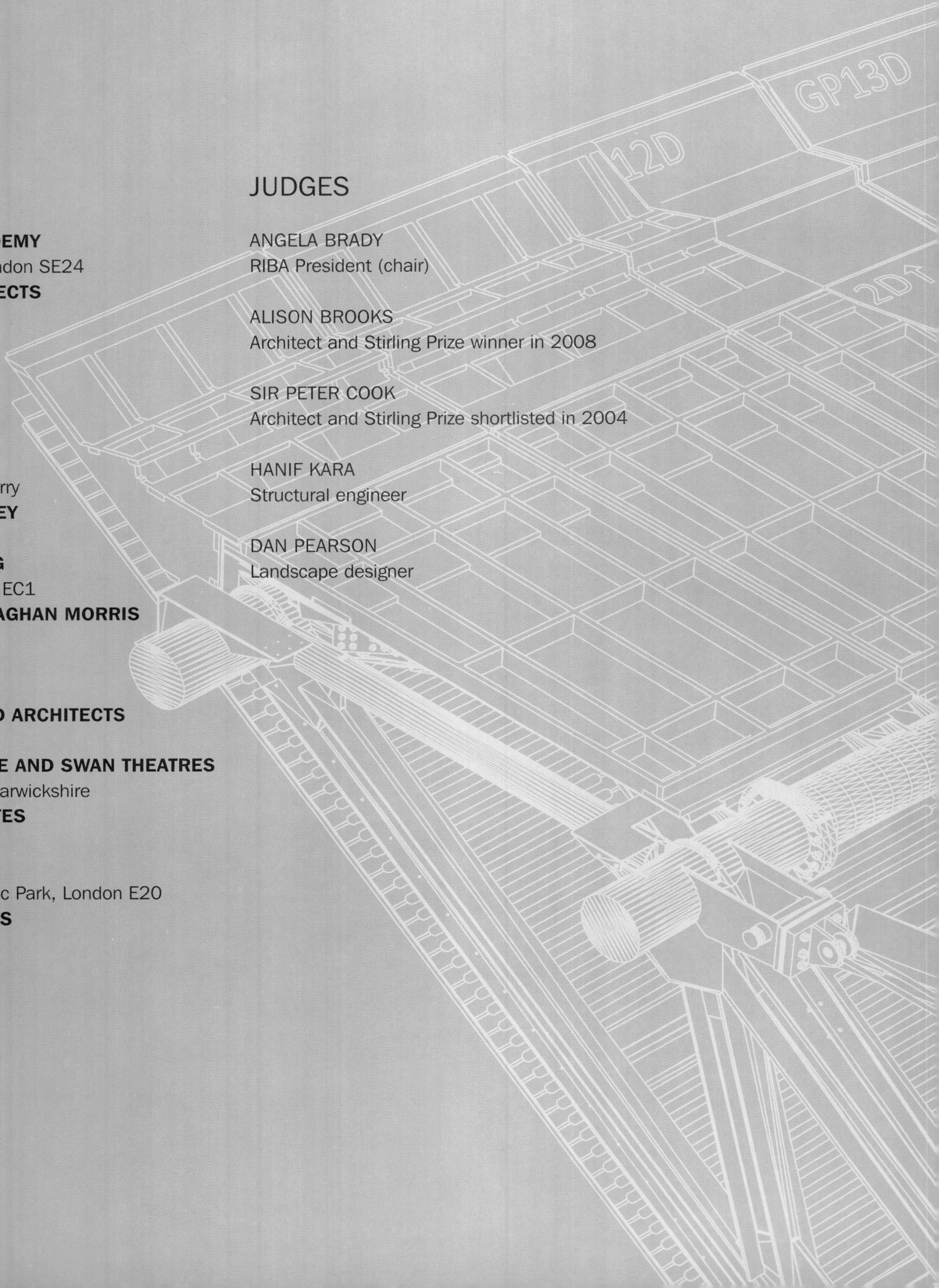

2011

WINNER

EVELYN GRACE ACADEMY
Shakespeare Road, London SE24

ZAHA HADID ARCHITECTS

Evelyn Grace is a truly extraordinary and original school, but in the opinion of the Stirling judges it is not just a one-off; rather, it is a scheme from which other schools architects can learn lessons.

The architect received a complex brief: four schools under a single academy umbrella, with the need to express both unity and independence. This is a large academy (for 1100 pupils) on a small site (just 1.4 hectares instead of the average 8 hectares). Without the luxury of a large greenfield site on which to scatter four discrete schools, Hadid opted for a 'stacking-and-packing' approach, yet because of the generosity of the accommodation and the ample provision of daylight in most areas, it does not feel crammed in.

This is narrative architecture that tells the story of the city, the neighbourhood and its student community as one moves through the site. Bringing renewed life to a long-neglected street, the new school announces itself with a ribbon of structural concrete that pulls away dynamically from the site edge, offering to the gritty surroundings an oasis of landscaping and playing fields. Having attracted our attention, Hadid leads us inside, where the architecture really starts to happen. Being a star architect allows a degree of licence, and here Hadid used her reputation entirely for good, challenging our expectations of what makes excellent academy architecture. For instance, there is no sign of the atrium that has become a trope in the design of so many academies. Instead, the money has wisely been spent on well-designed and lit classrooms, wide corridors, robust concrete elements and high-quality finishes to doors, ceilings and internal fixtures. The quality of the cladding and the internal glazed partitions is exceptional, and these will prove their cost-effectiveness over many years of use by 1000-plus students per day. The airy, flexible hall on two floors at the heart of the plan can be divided by acoustic screens into dining, teaching, assembly, drama and indoor-sport areas.

Curiously for a school that specializes in sport, the original site seemingly lacked any opportunity for significant outdoor games, but the architect responded with guile and intelligence, providing a multi-use Astroturf pitch that can be used either for football or simultaneously by different games requiring smaller playing areas. From an upper outdoor terrace one has clear views into the double gymnasium, kitted out with university-quality equipment. This is a cathedral-like space compared to most school gyms, filled with natural light

This sports-specialism academy features a 100-metre running track that sweeps under the building, dividing two wings at ground level.

CLIENT
Ark Schools

STRUCTURAL ENGINEER
Arup

CONTRACTOR
Mace Plus

CONTRACT VALUE
£37.5 million

IMAGES
Luke Hayes – VIEW (above; p. 163; p. 164; p. 165 bottom); Hufton + Crow – VIEW (opposite; p. 165 top)

2011

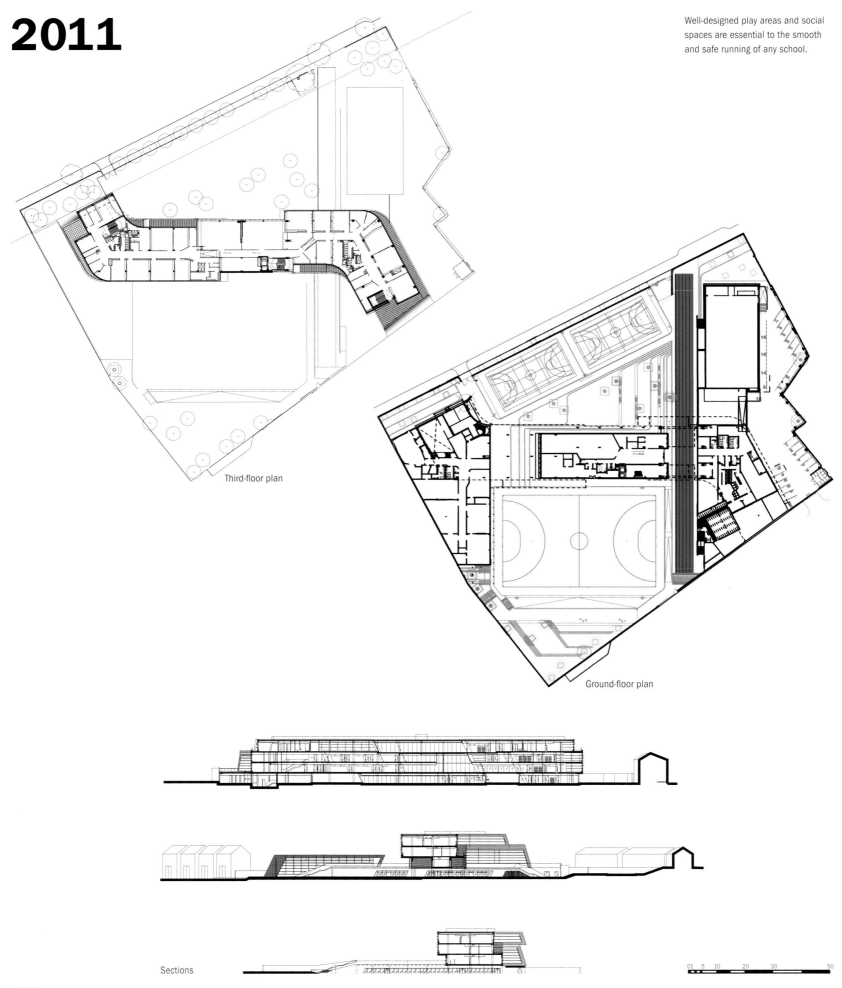

Third-floor plan

Ground-floor plan

Sections

01 5 10 20 30 50

2011

With space at a premium, play areas
are located not only at ground-floor
level but also here at first-floor level.

Inside, corridors are light and generous, discouraging bullying; classrooms are full of light, too.

from a great north wall of glazing that follows stairs down to the playing fields.

The two entrances to the site are joined by a bright-red 100-metre sprint track. The academy bridges the track at the 50-metre point, marking the doors in a playful, light-hearted manner. Why not make a running track an exciting landscape device for a school entrance?

The school is planned in the shape of a 'Z', with entrances and terraces woven into the wings. The two upper storeys of the school buildings rise out of a podium, which appears to reduce their height and mass in this area of small-scale housing. The podium roof also provides terraces that act as distinct gathering spaces for each school and age group in the morning and during breaks, thus reducing the bullying that inevitably occurs when children of different ages are forced together.

Internally, the academy provides good-quality, functional accommodation, with well-judged, exciting spatial moments as reminders that this is architecture and not just building: a fine stair detail here; a lovingly placed window midway up a stair there; benches designed into nooks and crannies; walls made of lockers, adding dabs of colour to the grey-and-white palette and opening on to corridors; with glazed clerestories allowing natural classroom light to fill the corridors. None of this is in any way at the expense of utility or value.

Speaking in 2016, Hadid said of her school: 'I think the academy programme was very good, and it was great to be able to concentrate on doing good architecture for a public programme. And it is very inspiring for the students and gives them knowledge about architecture, so they will be curious, whether consciously or not, about the space and the experience of it.'

The Stirling judges all agreed that the Evelyn Grace Academy establishes principles for future school-building: ultra-robust construction, a compact site strategy and excellent integrated landscaping, demonstrating the highest level of design for this neighbourhood. It has ingenious internal planning, uplifting spaces distributed throughout the building and beautifully designed internal sports facilities. This well-designed scheme encourages children to run into school in the morning: what finer endorsement could there be than that?

2011

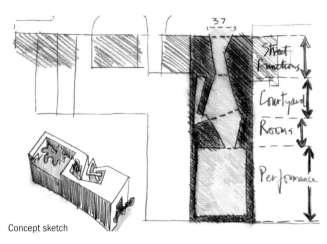

Concept sketch

An Gaeláras is a cultural centre that promotes the use and enjoyment of the Irish language. In Northern Ireland there is no such thing as just a building, and this one more than most is grounded in the thirty years of Troubles that beset this part of the island of Ireland. The project was funded by twenty different bodies north and south of the border, with money from both governments. Even so, funds were tight, and this has led to an inventiveness on the part of the architects, who revel in a richness of detail and colour.

Faced with an almost impossibly constricted site in a street of Georgian and Victorian terraces, further compromised by an electricity substation and a fire exit that largely occupy the frontage, O'Donnell + Tuomey has devised an intriguing and intricate vortex plan. With only one external elevation, three internal façades have been created. One is reminded of the same practice's Irish Film Centre in Dublin's Temple Bar, only here the streets have had to be built rather than conserved. Inside the cranked space, which is lit by a large, steeply sloping rooflight, it is as if one were in a twisting medieval lane in the old city. Shops, cafés and bars are all here and lead through to a theatre. At every turn, joy, inventiveness and a sense of pleasure may be found in the detailed exploration of form, light and materiality.

Above, teaching and office spaces, linked by stairs, bridges and platforms that circle and cross the internal courtyard, jostle for views. It is like exploring a castle, with secret stairways and surprising bolt-holes. The stairs appear and disappear as the route unfolds, inviting visitors to investigate the upper levels. It is a veritable architectural playground, but one that has been thoughtfully put together as a series of fractured spaces that draw the visitor into and up through the building.

AN GAELÁRAS
Great James Street, Derry

O'DONNELL + TUOMEY

The folded façade links two existing buildings, animating the street and allowing in extra light.

In scale, the building respects its neighbours, but materially it is very different, and speaks of culture as something that is aspirational as well as communal. The sense of the scheme as a sculptural intervention in a conventional street is enhanced by the use of beautiful board-marked concrete. The concrete adds gravitas and allows for the use of cheaper materials elsewhere: plywood, composition board and painted plaster.

The routes twist and turn like medieval alleyways in a hill town.

CLIENT
An Gaeláras

STRUCTURAL ENGINEER
Albert Fry Associates

SERVICES ENGINEER
IN2 Engineering

CONTRACTOR
JPM Contracts

CONTRACT VALUE
£2.8 million

IMAGES
Dennis Gilbert – VIEW

2011

THE ANGEL BUILDING
St John Street, London EC1

ALLFORD HALL MONAGHAN MORRIS

This speculative office space redefines the sector. An unremarkable 1980s office block has been transformed into a building of elegance and poise that has created new interiors of great refinement, and also contributes positively to life on the streets. The new building retains the original structure while infilling an old courtyard and adding offices on two edges. The additional floor area (now 25,000 square metres of lettable space instead of the original 15,000 square metres) is the key to increasing the building's rental value, thus unlocking the development.

The openness of the building produces an ambience that is quite different from that of most commercial buildings in central London. The entry sequence, with a publicly accessible café and lounge (the security is provided by smartly dressed people, not machines), sets civilized new standards for ways in which the atrium form can be used to animate a commercial ground floor as well as simply letting in light. A finely executed and generous 3-metre grid of *in-situ* concrete fins and beams (instead of the usual enslaving 1.5 metres) rises up to a gridded top light.

A magnificent polished black sculptural piece by McChesney Architects, *Out of the Strong Came Forth Sweetness*, looks like thick black treacle poured from the back of a spoon. It adds drama and counterpoint to the Kahnian gravitas of the atrium. The top storey opens out on to a roof terrace of such generous proportions and with such good fixtures and fittings that it has the feel of a luxury hotel, not a commercial office. The offices as offered to tenants have no suspended ceilings, so that the thermal mass of the concrete is fully available. Displacement ventilation is supplied through vents in the floor and drawn out through high-level concealed grilles. A rainwater-harvesting system produces the water for irrigation of the landscape and for flushing the toilets. This building is all about performance, but the most sustainable aspect of the project is the retention

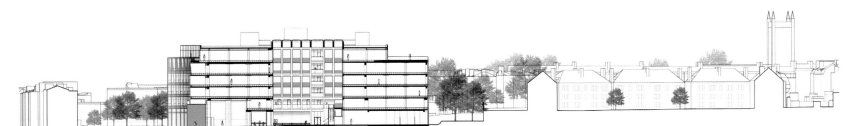

Sections

Opposite, top and left: The Angel has real street presence, holding its own against big-beast neighbours of brick and terracotta, and holding up a mirror to them.

Opposite, bottom: Less of a lobby, more public square – with its own public art.

CLIENT
Derwent London

STRUCTURAL ENGINEER
Adams Kara Taylor

SERVICES ENGINEER
Norman Disney & Young

CONTRACTOR
BAM Construct UK

CONTRACT VALUE
£72 million

IMAGES
Timothy Soar

of the previous structure's concrete frame, which accounts for a massive saving of CO_2 and reduced the budget by £350 per square metre.

It is to the huge credit of Derwent London and its architect, AHMM, that they created such high-end speculative office space and let it so successfully in a time of recession. The project offers an idea of how building and working in the city might become more dignified.

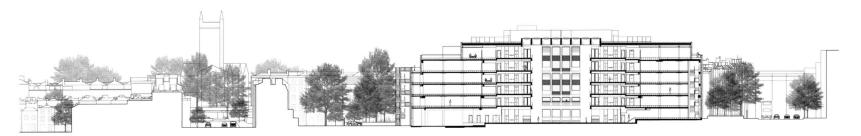

SHORTLISTED

MUSEUM FOLKWANG
Essen, Germany

DAVID CHIPPERFIELD ARCHITECTS

CLIENT
Neubau Museum Folkwang Essen on
behalf of the Alfried Krupp von Bohlen
und Halbach-Stiftung

STRUCTURAL ENGINEERS/
    CONTRACTORS
Pühl und Becker; Seroneit und
Schneider

SERVICES ENGINEER
Giesen-Gillhoff-Loomans

CONTRACT VALUE
Confidential

IMAGES
Christian Richters – VIEW

Right and opposite, top: David
Chipperfield's work links to the old
museum with no level change, and
maintains its architectural principles
with an ensemble of six structures and
four interior courtyards.

Opposite, centre and bottom: The
galleries and courts are mirror images
of each other, sharing proportions
and light.

Ground-floor plan

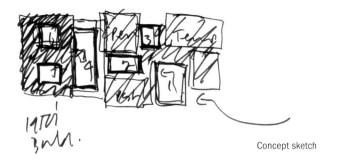

Concept sketch

Museum Folkwang is a breathtakingly accomplished design located in Essen, in the far-from-rural Ruhr. The brief was simple: to provide a home to match in architectural terms the artistic quality of one of the best collections of twentieth-century art in Germany. A predecessor museum was badly bombed during the Second World War and reopened in 1960; since then, the museum has been a meeting room for the city as well as a gallery of nineteenth- and twentieth-century art. David Chipperfield's new and impressive building continues that democratic tradition with its understated elegance and beauty.

The existing museum was in a handsomely simple late-1950s Miesian building designed by the city architects, and allowed passers-by to look in from the street and see the Van Goghs. Unfortunately, it had been extended in the 1980s by a building that had dated quickly and worn badly. The major move by Chipperfield was deciding on a podium to level off a sloping site and form the stone base for the new buildings, which replace and match the footprint of the 1980s museum. The result is a rather grand approach from the city via a series of ramps and staircases. Inside are genuinely uplifting, light-filled public spaces, offering a serene yet mesmeric mixture of inward-looking courtyards and views out.

The main external cladding is of large panels of crushed recycled glass, giving a shimmering translucent finish that has more of the qualities of alabaster than of glass. Inside, carefully detailed top-lighting systems blend natural and artificial light in galleries that are capable of being completely blacked out. The museum's director wanted natural light even at the cost of unevenness: for him, changes of light are better than a series of perfectly lit rooms. The entrance hall is conceived as an open interior courtyard with a café, restaurant and bookshop. The scheme also comprises a library and reading room, a multifunctional hall, art stores and restoration workshops.

Museum Folkwang was described by no less an authority than Paul J. Sachs, co-founder of the Museum of Modern Art in New York, as 'the most beautiful museum in the world'. That was in 1932. The following year the Nazis came to power, and much of the Museum Folkwang's 'degenerate' art was sold off or appropriated. Now, once again the museum is living up to its billing, thanks to the skill and inspiration of Chipperfield and his Berlin team.

2011

ROYAL SHAKESPEARE AND SWAN THEATRES
Stratford-upon-Avon, Warwickshire

BENNETTS ASSOCIATES

CLIENT
Peter Wilson, Royal Shakespeare
Company

STRUCTURAL ENGINEER
Buro Happold

THEATRE CONSULTANT
Charcoalblue

CONTRACTOR
Mace

CONTRACT VALUE
£60 million

IMAGES
Peter Cook – VIEW

Right: It was a bold move to house a
Globe-like theatre behind Elisabeth
Scott's listed modernist façade.

Below: Old and new mingle on
the Stratford skyline and in the
ambulatory.

In Stratford-upon-Avon, the relationship between theatre and town has long been fraught. Local feeling put paid to Erick van Egeraat's highly individualistic attempt in 1998 to replace Elisabeth Scott's 1930s theatre in its idyllic riverside setting. Instead the town council listed her Art Deco façade and foyer, according them Grade II* status. The new brief called for the rebuilding of the larger theatre to form a new 1000-seat thrust-stage auditorium, plus new facilities for actors and audience, all within an urban masterplan.

When Scott designed her theatre, Art Deco and cinema were twin design beacons. The legacy of the former is a number of rooms that have been lovingly restored and sympathetically fitted. The influence of the latter led to a wide fan-shaped auditorium with acoustics that murdered the actors' voices. That has changed utterly. Bennetts retained the rear wall, however, and this decision has produced the most successful part of the scheme: the carefully crafted spaces, now used for projection and circulation, in the voids between the back wall of the old theatre and the back wall of the new one. A small row of seats remains in place on the retained wall to show just how far from the stage the back seats used to be: 27 metres, compared with 15 metres today.

The new thrust-stage auditorium works extraordinarily well. It is robust, rough even. It has a Globe-like feel and an exciting atmosphere. It is historic in its references and contemporary in its design. The acoustics are superb. This is a good working theatre, not a precious one.

The tower works as both marker and viewing platform in a flat, low-lying town, and it brings into the theatre people who would not consider watching a play. But it too makes a historic reference. The old Victorian theatre featured a tower of identical height, the purpose of which was not viewing but fire-fighting. Sadly, the massive head-tank it contained did not stop the fire in 1926 that destroyed most of the building and led to Scott's flawed masterpiece.

Of Bennetts' work, one local told the Stirling judges: 'I love the stripped-backness of it, and I love the idea of reusing so many of the materials of the old theatre. They've recycled the boards trodden by Gielgud, Olivier and Richardson in the foyers. You can almost see the blood, the sweat and the tears that went into those old productions.'

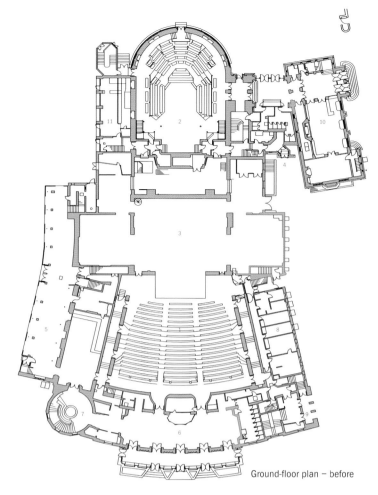

KEY
1 Royal Shakespeare Company
2 Swan Theatre
3 Stage and wing spaces
4 Stage door
5 Restaurant extension
6 Scott Foyer
7 Fountain Staircase
8 Offices
9 Balcony entrance
10 Library and Reading Room
11 Green Room

Ground-floor plan – before

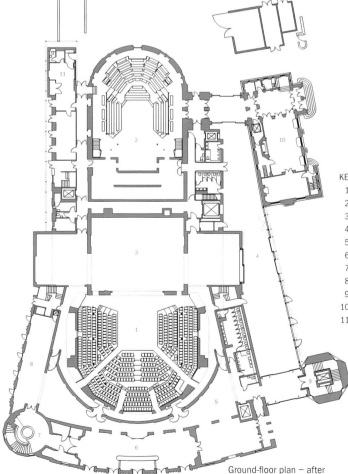

KEY
1 Royal Shakespeare Company
2 Swan Theatre
3 Stage and wing spaces
4 Colonnade
5 Foyer void
6 Scott Foyer
7 Fountain Staircase
8 Café
9 Theatre Tower
10 Library and Reading Room
11 Stage door

Ground-floor plan – after

2011

THE VELODROME
Queen Elizabeth Olympic Park, London E20

HOPKINS ARCHITECTS

Below and opposite, top: The timber bowl is a structure of great beauty and tactility.

Opposite, bottom: Even with the Velodrome's seating capacity of 6000, no spectator sits far from the track.

CLIENTS
London Organising Committee of the Olympic and Paralympic Games; Olympic Delivery Authority

STRUCTURAL ENGINEER
Expedition

SERVICES ENGINEER
BDSP Partnership

CONTRACTOR
ISG

CONTRACT VALUE
Confidential

IMAGES
Richard Davies (opposite); Anthony Palmer (below)

Quietly located at the north end of the Olympic Park masterplan, the Velodrome exudes elegance and simplicity. The very shape of the building signals the track itself, a continuous, sinuous form that seems to pre-empt and explain the movement of the sport it celebrates.

The site was a rubbish tip for the area of West Ham, and was referred to as Fridge Mountain. The mountain remains (this is the highest point of the Olympic Park and a fitting platform for the majestic, low-slung building), the land remediated and home now also to a switchback BMX track, a 1.6-kilometre road-cycle circuit, and 6 kilometres of mountain-bike trails. The project's legacy is already assured.

The building is made of three elements: the roof, the concourse and the plinth. The glazed concourse separates the curve of the larch-clad roof soffit and the concrete and landscaping of the plinth. The plinth contains all the service spaces and the normal legacy entrance. In Games mode, the lower ground areas housed concession and hospitality facilities. The approach from the plinth up to the concourse and the arena, via a well-detailed staircase, is modest and low-key, and the drama of the upper space is held back. In legacy mode, the concourse supports café facilities that look out over the landscape to the south.

Internally, the material palette is extremely well controlled, and fine *in-situ* concrete abounds. The material and visual emphasis is on the beauty and colour of the timber track, a surface that is constantly and lovingly vacuumed and cleaned.

The cable-net roof seems to hang in space, detached from the ground by the glazed concourse. While the roof is a significant engineering achievement, it does not shout its presence; instead it is turned through 90 degrees from the track from which it takes its shape, and sits low over the bowl, adding drama and focus to the cycling. The arena is an extremely intimate space, given the seating capacity of 6000. No seat is far away from the track; indeed, some spectators are within touching distance of the cyclists.

The building consummately delivers a simple idea, carrying it out beautifully and efficiently. It is an enormous credit to both the client and the design team that the effect is one of effortlessness and grace. The plan is an exercise in clarity of purpose and rigorous resolution, while the form is, quite simply, memorable.

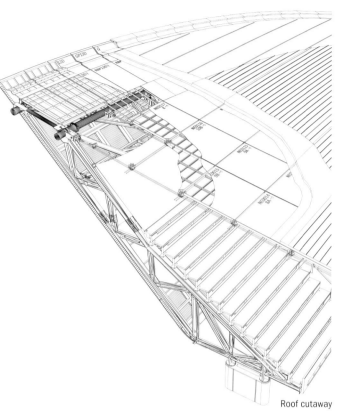

Roof cutaway

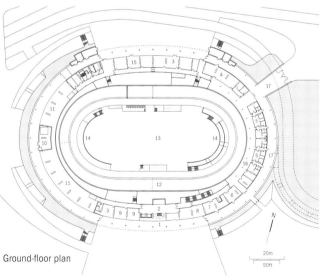

Ground-floor plan

20m
50ft

KEY

1 Main entrance
2 Reception
3 Office
4 Gym
5 Changing room
6 Bike hire
7 Workshop
8 Retail
9 Meeting room

10 Rainwater harvesting
11 Storage undercroft
12 Track
13 Infield
14 Access ramp from basement
15 Seminar/conference space
16 Internal circulation
17 Circulation to external
   cycle tracks

2012

WINNER

SAINSBURY LABORATORY,
UNIVERSITY OF CAMBRIDGE
Bateman Street, Cambridge
STANTON WILLIAMS

SHORTLIST

THE HEPWORTH WAKEFIELD
Wakefield, West Yorkshire
DAVID CHIPPERFIELD ARCHITECTS

LYRIC THEATRE
Ridgeway Street, Belfast
O'DONNELL + TUOMEY

MAGGIE'S GLASGOW,
GARTNAVEL GENERAL HOSPITAL
Great Western Road, Glasgow
OMA

NEW COURT
St Swithin's Lane, London EC4
OMA WITH ALLIES AND MORRISON

OLYMPIC STADIUM
Queen Elizabeth Olympic Park, London E20
POPULOUS

JUDGES

SIR NICHOLAS GRIMSHAW
Architect, former President of the Royal
Academy and Stirling Prize shortlisted
in 2001 and 2008 (chair)

NAOMI CLEAVER
Designer, writer and broadcaster

HILDE DAEM
Architect

JOANNA VAN HEYNINGEN
Architect

SIR MARK JONES
Master of St Cross College, Oxford,
and former Director of the Victoria
and Albert Museum

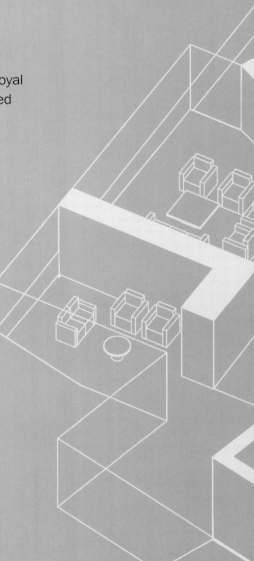

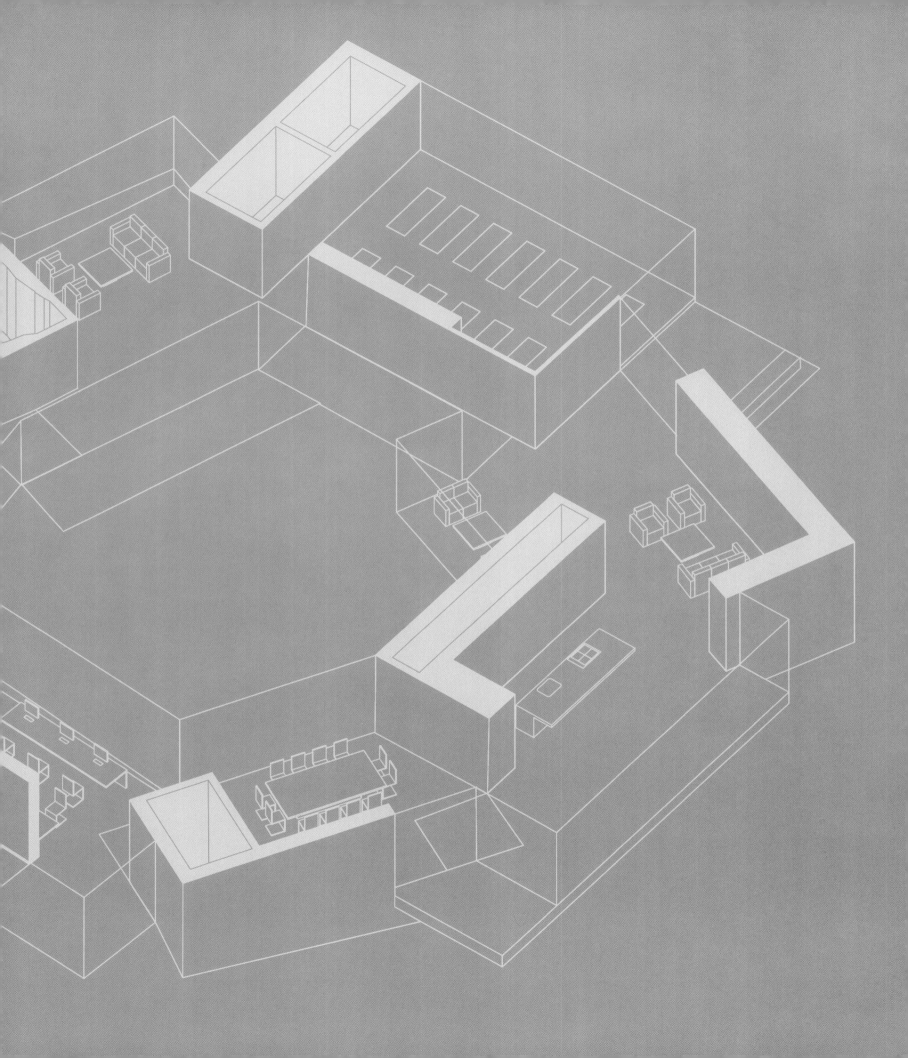

The formal front elevation of the
Sainsbury Laboratory addresses
the city of Cambridge.

SAINSBURY LABORATORY, UNIVERSITY OF CAMBRIDGE
Bateman Street, Cambridge

STANTON WILLIAMS

In the Sainsbury Laboratory, Stanton Williams has finally found the brief and the client that perfectly match its intelligent and finely considered architecture. An architectural promenade forms the heart of a building that celebrates botanical research through interaction, communication and a connection with nature. From the entrance, the building progresses from a grand, colonnaded façade to an open balcony and glazed public café, set within the university's Botanic Garden.

The front (or is it really the back?) addresses the city of Cambridge, represented by a row of three-storey terraced houses. To avoid overlooking (in either direction), a colonnade of creamy stone shades the scientists' offices and allows windows to be opened. Sustainability through flexibility in long-term use is achieved by an adaptable façade behind the limestone pillars, enabling these research spaces to grow and change as required by the scientists. This more formal, austere and closed elevation, with stone blades affording privacy as well as shading, announces that this is a place where serious work goes on. But as the building turns the corner away from the city, it unfurls, becoming more open, more transparent and public as it addresses the bucolic gardens.

Inside the entrance, the floor gently ramps down towards a crossroads in the street. Turn right for the auditorium; turn left for the meeting rooms; take the broad shallow stair down to the herbarium, where the collections that Charles Darwin sent back from his voyage on HMS *Beagle* are carefully stored; or take the stairs up to the laboratories, which are the heart of the building and its *raison d'être*. Here, at the upper level, the scientists work on illuminated stages, with research and write-up areas forming the ends of two promenades, flanked by small spontaneous breakout areas with niche seating for sharing ideas and knowledge, and whiteboards for capturing inspiration.

Scientists are sometimes treated as the second-class citizens of the academic world, and they are notoriously

2012

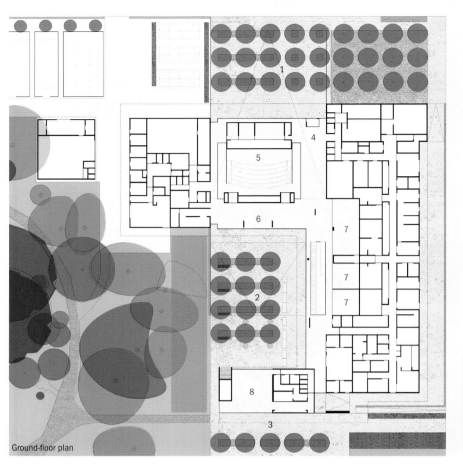

Ground-floor plan

KEY
1 Entry court
2 Central court
3 Café terrace
4 Main entrance
5 Lecture theatre
6 Internal street/Staff dining
7 Meeting rooms
8 Public café

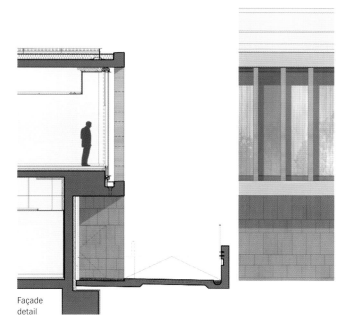

Façade
detail

undemanding when it comes to their working conditions, putting up with anything provided they are given the freedom and the technical facilities to enable them to get on with their research. It was the project's sponsor, David Sainsbury, who insisted that they deserved better, and that the university should recognize the importance of creating some of the world's best laboratory spaces in order to attract the world's best scientists. Now the university has both.

Despite the high energy demands of laboratories, the building has achieved a BREEAM rating of 'Excellent', aided by 1000 square metres of photovoltaic panels, a 100-cubic-metre rainwater tank for the irrigation of the glasshouse and plant growth chambers, and extensive natural lighting even in the laboratories. The top-lit labs are arranged on a single floor in an L-shape, encouraging interaction.

The brief called for a building that facilitated 'world-class science', but also stipulated that it should achieve

Inside, the clinical white lines of
the laboratories are softened by the
timber, the light and the shade of the
circulation spaces.

2012

CLIENT
University of Cambridge

STRUCTURAL ENGINEER
Adams Kara Taylor

SERVICES ENGINEER
Arup

CONTRACTOR
Kier Regional

CONTRACT VALUE
£69 million

IMAGES
Hufton + Crow – VIEW

The laboratories are arranged in such a way that interaction among scientists is positively encouraged.

'world-class architecture' – and in the context of a sensitive landscape setting: the Grade II-listed Botanic Garden. No permanent buildings were destroyed in the making of the laboratory, which occupies the site of greenhouses and sheds that served the garden, a ramshackle back-of-house area. The building bridges the private and the public domain in its provision of a fine, highly glazed café for the Botanic Garden. Here visitors can learn about the significance of the work in the labs and its contribution to the survival of our species, or just enjoy a coffee overlooking the garden where Darwin walked with his tutor John Stevens Henslow, discussing such matters. The café also overlooks the private collegiate courtyard, the fourth wall of which comprises scientifically important trees planted by Henslow himself.

This building mixes history and the contemporary, as well as serious science and its promotion, in an exciting new typology, juxtaposing spaces for research with spaces

for education, the private with the public, and the highly technological nurture of nature with the simple enjoyment of an extended Botanic Garden. It took a generous sponsor, a dedicated client and serious and sensitive architects to achieve all this, and each is to be equally commended.

Alan Stanton, the project director, told the Stirling judges: 'We have arranged the building so that we were able to get daylight into all the labs; it's really unusual for a lab to be daylit. The building also had to be open to the future and very adaptable. The courtyard was a way of capturing the space of the garden, and it also gave us the opportunity to have a twenty-first-century cloister around it, where scientists can move, walk and have conversations. Aside from the technical issues, one of the great challenges here was to create a community of scientists and get them to talk to one another about their work, because they all tend to work in separate compartments.'

The broken façades face the 'country'
– the courtyard and the gardens.

2012

THE HEPWORTH WAKEFIELD
Wakefield, West Yorkshire

DAVID CHIPPERFIELD ARCHITECTS

The promise of the building draws the visitor across an elegant entrance bridge, surrounded by all manner of strange rivercraft and motley post-industrial buildings. The gallery works beautifully within this varied and gritty context, suggesting that it both belongs and at the same time is something rather special. Its scale shifts as you approach; the carefully cast dusky mauve-grey concrete external forms make you want to stroke them. This is a building for all seasons, which is important given its riparian context: a horseshoe bend in the River Calder, the basin, the weir, the wharves, the bridge. And everywhere the urgent flow of water. The northern elevations rise sheer out of the waters, like a castle from a moat. It took a major piece of engineering just to get the project built: the river had to be dammed and the basin drained for six months while the foundations were dug. Constructed from pigmented *in-situ* concrete, the building is a conglomeration of differently sized trapezoidal blocks, each of different dimensions, grouped along the water's edge.

The programme is split horizontally between the ground floor and the first floor; the latter is used exclusively for exhibition space. The ground floor houses the shop, café, education room and offices, radiating out from the entrance space. The stair, wrapped in a beautiful, tactile grey MDF lining, takes the visitor up to the first-floor galleries. Here circulation takes the form of a promenade leading through an enfilade of rooms. Now the external morphology can be understood: each volume contains a single gallery. Ceilings slope to match the outer roofs, and no room is a parallelogram, meaning that each has a unique atmosphere. The long slit rooflight is a recurring theme that models each space, while the carefully placed windows serve to rest the eye and constantly locate the building against the context of Helmsley moor, the town hall, the weir and the Chantry Chapel of St Mary.

The major galleries house permanent displays of large-scale sculptures and plaster casts by Barbara Hepworth and other artists, as well as highly light-sensitive works on paper from the city of Wakefield's collection of British art. The remaining rooms host temporary exhibitions. The gallery is very focused and perfectly considered. It gives the sense of being made specifically for the work of Hepworth, while at the same time being very much of Yorkshire, grounded and granite-like. This is a life-affirming project on every level.

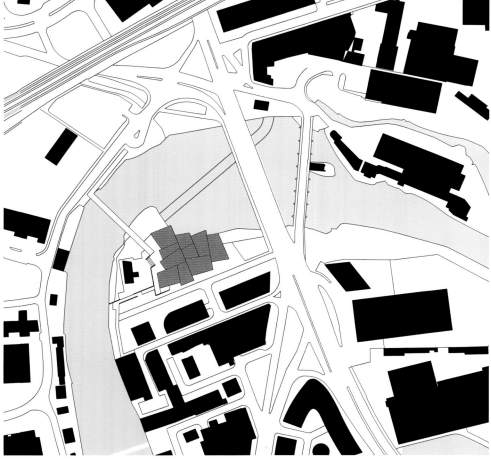

Site plan

Opposite and above: Powerful views of the 'castle' with its moat and drawbridge.

Left: All galleries are daylit, often by soft side light, and are capable of being reconfigured as black boxes.

CLIENT
Wakefield Council

STRUCTURAL/SERVICES ENGINEER
Ramboll UK

CONTRACTOR
Laing O'Rourke Northern

CONTRACT VALUE
£22.8 million

IMAGES
Iwan Baan (opposite; left);
Hélène Binet (above)

Idyllic Belfast, a post-Troubles city where the arts can, and do, flourish.

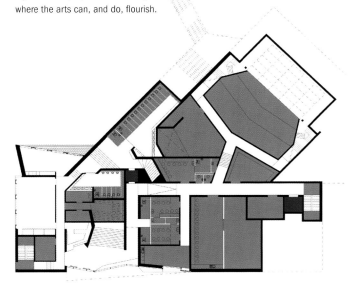

First-floor plan

LYRIC THEATRE
Ridgeway Street, Belfast

O'DONNELL + TUOMEY

CLIENT
Lyric Theatre

STRUCTURAL ENGINEER
Horgan Lynch

SERVICES ENGINEER
IN2 Engineering

CONTRACTOR
Gilbert Ash

CONTRACT VALUE
£18 million

IMAGES
Dennis Gilbert – VIEW

The new Lyric Theatre is a striking home for a theatre with a unique status in Belfast: it is the only one with its own company. The architects responded with gusto to the considerable design challenges of its location. The steeply sloping river frontage within a tightly-knit fabric of brick terraced houses presented a demanding agenda for a building type that requires large volumes to accommodate the auditorium, studio and rehearsal room. The Lyric Theatre meets that challenge admirably; the line of brick terraces seems to flow into the Lyric's façade in a gentle crescendo. The theatre is at once self-effacing and self-confident, deferential and assertive.

The lobby accommodates a box office that does its modest job: that of selling 389 tickets for the main house and up to 170 for the studio theatre. At the top of the first flight of stairs the space fans out into areas for gathering, drinking, eating and anticipating the performance. The concrete is gorgeous, the joinery immaculate. The tactility of this area leads to the enveloping, dark and dramatic volume of the main theatre itself. This is a democratic space with a single shallow rake: no one is more than sixteen rows back from the stage. The faceted walnut is rich aesthetically as well as acoustically. Its origami-like folds absorb and reflect back the actors' words in exact measures.

The theatre is a factory for making plays and its workforce – actors, stagehands, wardrobe and front-of-house staff – deserve decent working conditions. Seldom is back of house as well done as it is here. Theatres are normally designed for audiences, not actors, but at the Lyric the route from the well-appointed, restful green room, along corridors made of exactly the same materials as the public routes and lined with photographs of past productions, shows the hard-working actors the respect they deserve but so rarely receive.

Belfast now has what is in all but name the National Theatre of Northern Ireland. The Lyric is a tangible portion of the peace dividend, and it was the chosen venue in 2012 for HM The Queen and Northern Ireland's Deputy First Minister, Martin McGuinness, to meet for the first time and shake hands. The quality of the interior spaces, the sensitive response to a challenging site and the expansion of the Lyric's ability to function behind the scenes make this a stunning accomplishment and a pleasurable building in which to spend time.

The dramatic stair and the areas for gathering lead to the enveloping, dark and spectacular space of the theatre itself.

2012

SHORTLISTED

MAGGIE'S GLASGOW, GARTNAVEL GENERAL HOSPITAL
Great Western Road, Glasgow

OMA

CLIENT
Maggie's

STRUCTURAL ENGINEER
Sinclair Knight Merz

SERVICES ENGINEER
K.J. Tait Engineers

LANDSCAPE ARCHITECTS
Lily Jencks with Harrison Stevens

CONTRACTOR
Dunne

CONTRACT VALUE
Confidential

IMAGES
Philippe Ruault

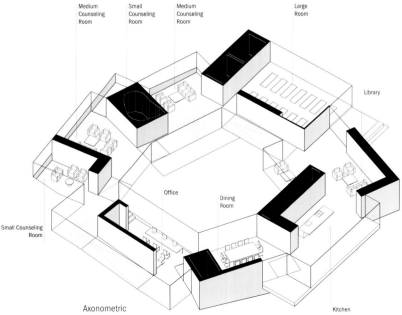

Medium Counseling Room · Small Counseling Room · Medium Counseling Room · Large Room · Library · Small Counseling Room · Office · Dining Room · Kitchen

Axonometric

Glasgow's new Maggie's Centre, like its sister projects, sets out to provide a place where people can feel welcome, at home and cared for – a haven. This seems to be a tall order, considering its setting amid austere and soulless hospital buildings. Designed as a single storey, this Maggie's Centre strikes the visitor with its predominance of glazed walls in a doughnut plan. The circuit is fully glazed on both elevations: one looking out to the hospital, and the internal elevation overlooking the central courtyard. Simultaneously one is aware of a series of interlocking rectangular spaces that lead away in a jagged, gently ramped circuit.

Much of Rem Koolhaas's work can be seen as lifelong battle against the corridor. His best buildings are in fact a series of spaces around which the building happens. But here counselling requires as much privacy as treatment (which takes place only in the behemoth of the cancer hospital next door), so doors are a necessity. They slide shut to enclose discrete counselling rooms or private nooks and corners, or open to create circulation space. And then there is the required set piece of every Maggie's: the kitchen table, designed and made by local artisans. There are no timetables here and no agenda. The centre's users simply turn up to be welcomed with a cup of tea, and are encouraged to relax ('to exhale', in client Laura Lee's words) the moment they walk through the sliding door.

There is a surprisingly rich variety of materials and skills on display, with a particularly pleasing flush inlaid timber-and-concrete ceiling. As in the case of the architects and all the consultants, the contractor gave its time for free, yet it was more than willing to experiment with the ceiling until it worked to perfection. The building is curiously introvert and extrovert at the same time. Nearly all the spaces relate to the landscape, which was designed by Maggie's daughter; either to the grassy banks, tree trunks and foliage outside, or to the interior grassed mound, visible through floor-to-ceiling glass. There is a medley of different spaces and materials, but this is a masterful composition in a highly efficient plan. Despite its apparent contradictions – introspective/extrovert, transparent/private, personal/communal, active/calm – it achieves a connectedness, transparency and an informal charm that meets the brief admirably to offer an uplifting refuge to those dealing with cancer, be they sufferers or their family and friends.

The nurturing heart of Maggie's: the top-lit meditation room (opposite), one of the bracelet of rooms that link hands around the central landscaped courtyard (below).

Left: In common with most Maggie's Centres, the entrance politely invites you in, but does not demand that you step inside.

2012

CLIENT
Rothschild

FIT-OUT ARCHITECT
Pringle Brandon

STRUCTURAL/SERVICES ENGINEER
Arup

CONTRACTOR
Lendlease

CONTRACT VALUE
Confidential

IMAGES
OMA (right); OMA by Philippe Ruault
(opposite)

NEW COURT
St Swithin's Lane, London EC4

OMA WITH ALLIES AND MORRISON

Rothschild has occupied the New Court site on St Swithin's Lane in the City of London since 1809. This new corporate headquarters, the fourth iteration of Rothschild's London home, not only consolidates the bank's previously dispersed facilities within one building, but also makes a number of important urban moves, reinstating the historic visual connection between St Swithin's and Christopher Wren's neighbouring church of St Stephen Walbrook, hidden from public view by previous New Court developments. OMA and Allies and Morrison worked closely for eighteen months with Peter Rees, City planner, and his team, adjusting the design in order to achieve planning consent for a building twice the height of any of its neighbours, including Mansion House and the Bank of England.

The new building is organized into a central cube capped with a smaller rooftop tower, surrounded by three adjoining annexes that contain the main circulation and allow uninterrupted office floors within the central cube, with abundant daylight and views out to the City. The central cube is lifted above St Swithin's Lane by a series of pilotis that create a wider cloistered edge and a raised covered entrance square. This sequence of new public realm and vistas gives something back to improve the quality of the everyday life and streetscape of the City, and simultaneously lends a quiet public presence to this previously most private of institutions.

The attention to detail and the combination of materials provide a sense of understated elegance, heightened by the considered contrast between original paintings and artefacts, beautifully displayed and lit in vitrines, and quirky, super-scale graphics and photographic blow-ups. OMA's interest in fabrics and print is evident everywhere on the upper floors, where rooms for meetings, dining and functions are decorated with a mix of images: screen-printed, woven into tapestries or etched on to metal. All images are drawn from Rothschild's collection of fine and decorative arts and archives. The latter are stored on-site in a book-lined room with oak joinery by Robert Thompson, the Mouseman of Kilburn, North Yorkshire, whose trademark is a carved mouse on every piece to leave the workshop. The archive opens directly on to the entrance square, its intimacy contrasting with the generosity of the volume that houses the lobby, the lively acoustic of which is somewhat softened by the full-length drapes by OMA. The City has a new and surprising masterpiece.

Opposite: The two City towers serving God and Mammon: St Stephen Walbrook in front of New Court, both objects of subtle beauty.

Below: The simplicity of the plan belies the richness of the interiors, which are hung with artworks both old and – in the lobby – contemporary.

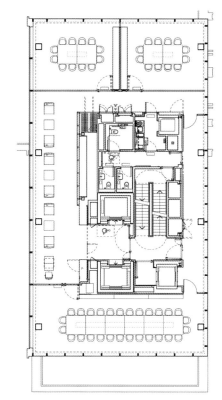

Level 14 plan

2012

OLYMPIC STADIUM
Queen Elizabeth Olympic Park, London E20

POPULOUS

CLIENTS
London Organising Committee of
the Olympic and Paralympic Games
(LOCOG); Olympic Delivery Authority

STRUCTURAL/SERVICES ENGINEER
Buro Happold

LANDSCAPE ARCHITECT
Hyland Edgar Driver

CONTRACTOR
Sir Robert McAlpine

CONTRACT VALUE
Confidential

IMAGES
LOCOG (far right); Olympic Delivery
Authority (right); Morley von Sternberg
(below)

The hosting of the 2012 Olympic Games condensed thirty
years of urban regeneration into just a decade, producing
a series of new facilities in the largest new park to be built
in London for more than a century. Central to the vision for
2012 was the creation of not only world-class venues for the
period of the Games, but also ones that formed a legacy of
sustainable facilities for future use by the people of London.

The design of the new stadium, which formed the
centrepiece of the Olympic and Paralympic Games, embraces
this ambition: the venue seated 80,000 spectators for the
main track-and-field events and ceremonies, and is also
capable of being transformed into a smaller athletics stadium
accommodating 25,000 people or a football ground with a
capacity of up to 60,000. The design clearly expresses the
main elements of the stadium, distinguishing between the
white main structural elements (the horizontal members are
lengths of leftover Russian gas pipe), the black secondary
structures and the precast concrete of the seating tiers and
plinth. The result is a striking and legible ensemble. The
structure is designed so that it can be dismantled to form the
smaller legacy venue, with the remaining elements capable
of being recycled. The demountable nature of the structure
is expressed through the simple and elegant detailing of its
many connections and components.

The organization focuses on the ease of movement of
the large numbers of people who used the stadium during

the Games. Spectators approached via a bridge across the canalized river that all but makes an island of the site. The water forms a natural barrier and means that security on the 'island' could be less rigorous. The stadium wrap comprises narrow sails of PVC that offer wind protection at the upper levels and are twisted towards the ground to expose the gradated colours of the London Olympics and to allow access from the arrival plinth. The plinth runs round the full perimeter of the stadium, giving level wheelchair access. Because the bowl is cut into the ground, the entry point is halfway up, making access easier for all and providing clear sight lines. Movement is also simplified because the concourse is free of food outlets, which are instead located in temporary pods outside the stadium. User satisfaction measured during the Olympics and Paralympics recorded that more than 97 per cent were pleased with the facilities.

Opposite, top and above: Superbowl: the cauldron of the stadium offered up to the City of London and, inside the bowl, some of the best views in modern sport.

Opposite, bottom: A section in photographic form, showing the structure of the stadium.

2013

WINNER

ASTLEY CASTLE
Nuneaton, Warwickshire
WITHERFORD WATSON MANN ARCHITECTS

SHORTLIST

BISHOP EDWARD KING CHAPEL
Cuddesdon, Oxfordshire
NÍALL McLAUGHLIN ARCHITECTS

GIANT'S CAUSEWAY VISITOR CENTRE
Bushmills, County Antrim
HENEGHAN PENG ARCHITECTS

NEWHALL BE
Harlow, Essex
ALISON BROOKS ARCHITECTS

PARK HILL PHASE 1
South Street, Park Hill, Sheffield
HAWKINS\BROWN WITH STUDIO EGRET WEST

UNIVERSITY OF LIMERICK MEDICAL SCHOOL, STUDENT HOUSING AND BUS SHELTER
Limerick, Ireland
GRAFTON ARCHITECTS

JUDGES

STEPHEN HODDER
RIBA President and Stirling Prize winner in 1996 (chair)

DAME VIVIAN DUFFIELD
Philanthropist and Chair of the Clore Duffield Foundation

TOM DYCKHOFF
Journalist and broadcaster

SHEILA O'DONNELL
Architect and Stirling Prize shortlisted in 1999, 2005, 2011 and 2012

PAUL WILLIAMS
Architect and Stirling Prize winner in 2012

WINNER

ASTLEY CASTLE
Nuneaton, Warwickshire

WITHERFORD WATSON MANN ARCHITECTS

The brief from the Landmark Trust was to provide a contemporary house within the footprint of the ruins of a twelfth-century fortified manor destroyed by fire in 1978. The decision to put the bedrooms and bathrooms on the ground floor and the communal spaces above makes the experience of the house very special. The sculptural central staircase is the pivot around which the bedrooms are organized, and leads to an open-plan living space with views over the ancient ruins and moated gardens. Perhaps the most impressive spaces are outdoors: the ruins of the Tudor and Jacobean wings. The experience and reading of the remains are enhanced by the new interventions. The architects have developed a set of carefully considered rules and methodology for new construction abutting the existing structure.

The challenge of how to be resolutely of the present age while simultaneously embracing the past is one of the most complex problems that architects have had to face throughout history. It is also the one that has caused the most dispute. Astley Castle resolves that argument with beauty, intelligence and a rigour that runs through to the smallest of details. There is, of course, great romance to a ruined castle. This, however, can be as much hindrance as help to the architect seeking to give the ruin a future, a highly pragmatic one at that, as a holiday home. Witherford Watson Mann has managed at once to respect the past, to be gentle in its relationship, while at the same time not being afraid to make its architectural presence felt – and with some force. It has dealt with Astley's ruins with discernment and practicality, while adding to them with a contemporary architecture that is rich, visually beautiful and tactile. The architects have responded intuitively to the site, working with the client throughout the process on a voyage of discovery, to give the castle its new form.

Not just saving but darning, as the poet Stevie Smith might have said. Witherford Watson Mann has darned together old and new so that, deliberately, the joins show – but also the skill.

2013

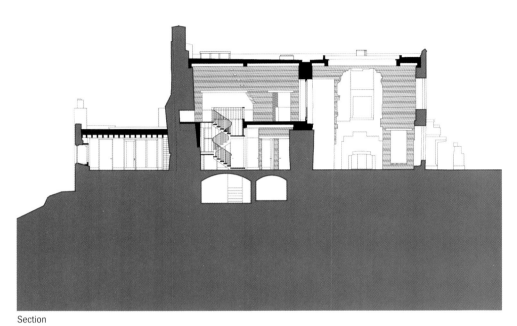

Section

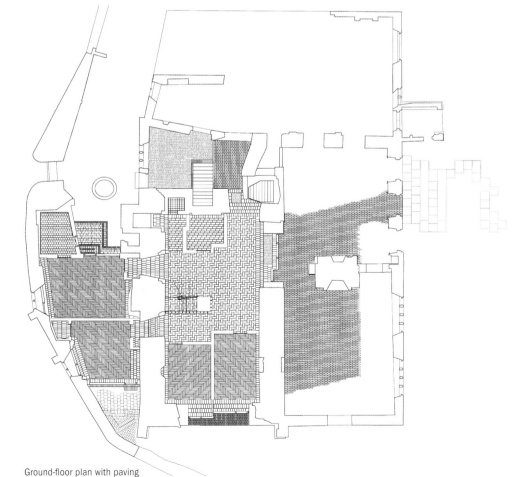

Ground-floor plan with paving

The result darns together not only the present and the past, but also the head and the heart with a complexity and deftness that are truly appreciated only when one is within the building itself. This is a scheme that constantly reveals itself both inside and out. For this, we have to thank the client, Anna Keay, director of the Landmark Trust, who was willing to be extremely ambitious in her commissioning. Because, in the end, all great architecture comes down to a conversation between client and architect, between history and the present.

Steve Witherford, project director, told the Stirling jury: 'We thought the colours and the patina were so interesting, but not in a romantic way. In a way, the ravage of the fire and the destruction are interesting on a human level, so we didn't want to tidy it up too much. The new architecture is the thing that stabilizes the ruin. What we did was to make a new ruin, and we wanted all the broken edges, all the destruction, to be apparent. So all the new brickwork is built on medieval footings, binding all the masonry together. And then, to make sure the new walls would move like the medieval walls, we back-filled them with rubble that we had collected from the demolition.'

Anna Keay said: 'It shouldn't be that you have to do either just a faithful restoration or one that leaves your ravaged ruin as an inconvenient thing in the background of some sort of funky new development; it should be possible

Above: The grand salon, now an open court for al fresco dining, with its original medieval hearth and chimney intact and still in working order.

Opposite: A view of an end elevation demonstrates the painstaking work of the architects.

2013

Internally, the only major additions to the found and saved materials of brick and stone are new timber elements.

to do something that is both old and new. What we wanted, and what Steve has been so brilliant in achieving, was not to erase the ruination of Astley Castle, because it is so eloquent about its own history.'

The critic Oliver Wainwright, a man unaccustomed to enthusing about high-end accommodation, wrote in *The Guardian* in July 2013: '[Witherford Watson Mann's] addition is neither the usual insertion of a "look at me, I'm the modern bit" glass box, nor is it the kind of understated invisible mending so beloved of conservation architects. Knitting walls of brick and timber into the ravaged stonework, the architects have crafted a layered sequence of domestic rooms that revel in framing views and overlapping spaces, inside and out – giving the bewitching sense of a contemporary house enclosed by the jacket of the original ruin.'

Joseph Rykwert, recipient of the Royal Gold Medal in 2014, said of this project: 'There is no comparable recovery of an ancient monument anywhere in this country, and very few elsewhere.' The question of conservation and finding new uses for buildings whose original function has disappeared is extremely pertinent today, not only because of the economic climate, but also because Britain is a country that wears its past resolutely on its sleeve. History is central to our national identity. This is a clever and robust response to the issue, instead of one that is over-cautious or that clashes inappropriately. Here history becomes a living, energetic force.

CLIENT
The Landmark Trust

STRUCTURAL ENGINEER
Price & Myers

SERVICES ENGINEER
BDP

CONTRACTOR
William Anelay

CONTRACT VALUE
£1.35 million

IMAGES
Hélène Binet (p. 196; p. 197;
p. 199; opposite, top; right);
J. Miller (opposite, bottom);
Philip Vile (p. 198)

2013

BISHOP EDWARD KING CHAPEL
Cuddesdon, Oxfordshire

NÍALL McLAUGHLIN ARCHITECTS

For all the chapel's empathy with its historic surroundings, this is a new piece of work, speaking of its time in the same way as Basil Spence's Coventry Cathedral.

The chapel was built for the community of Ripon College Cuddesdon, a theological college, and the nuns of a small religious order, the Sisters of Begbroke. The project aspires to provide a place of worship that meets the needs of both individual and communal prayer in a collegiate seating arrangement.

This small chapel is a significant triumph. The entrance is positioned between the bell tower and a spectacularly ancient beech tree that previously dominated this open courtyard of the college. The building sits amid its own ring of mature trees and defies its diminutive scale to provide an uplifting spiritual space of great potency.

This is a materially rich scheme. The simple oval, stone-clad form appears set deep in the lawns of the college and, as it rises, the surface texture of Clipsham stone changes scale from a base of fine ashlar to a middle of cropped walling in a coursed dog-tooth bond, and finally to a capping ring of tall, stone-finned windows that cast an ethereal light into the interior. Inside, the wall and roof structure are separated, offering the visitor the experience of chancing upon a glade in the woods. The subtlety of the spatial differentiation between the outer path – accessing specific views, a sacristy and side chapel – and the shallow-dished central space, where the eye is drawn up by the verticals of the structural trees to the interconnected canopy overhead, is deeply moving.

Material finishes are all lightened, bringing them gently together as a close family of off-white textures, so that they do not compete with one another and with the simplicity of the space. Furniture is simple, elegant and functional. The small side chapel for the sisters and the vestry are quietly top-lit and furnished in a way that resonates brilliantly with the main chapel.

This is a richly rewarding building to visit once, but it merits being seen in different lights and at different times. Only then can one appreciate the way daylight has been harnessed to articulate the chapel structure and interior in an ever-changing dance with the time of day and the season – a fitting backdrop to the rhythms of prayer and service. In this sense, the scheme has managed to meet its brief with a lyrical grace that sets it apart. This is a church for all seasons and serves equally all the diverse branches of the Anglican Church.

Inside, the pale wood and top light give the chapel a calm and appropriately monastic air.

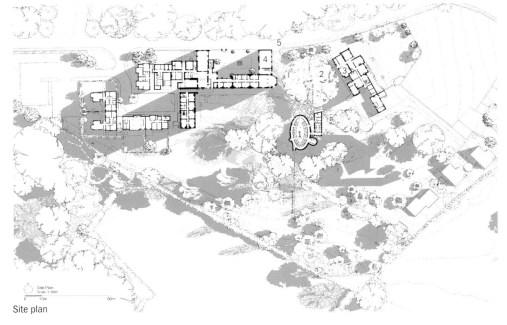

Site plan

CLIENT
Ripon College Cuddesdon and
Community of St John Baptist

STRUCTURAL ENGINEER
Price & Myers

SERVICES ENGINEER
Synergy Consulting Engineers

CONTRACTOR
Beard Construction

CONTRACT VALUE
£2.03 million

IMAGES
Níall McLaughlin

KEY

1 New chapel
2 Existing beech tree
3 College House
4 Linden Building
5 Entrance to college

2013

GIANT'S CAUSEWAY VISITOR CENTRE
Bushmills, County Antrim

HENEGHAN PENG ARCHITECTS

CLIENT
National Trust

STRUCTURAL ENGINEER
Arup

SERVICES ENGINEER
Bennett Robertson

LANDSCAPE DESIGN
Heneghan Peng Architects;
Mitchell + Associates

CONTRACTOR
Gilbert Ash

CONTRACT VALUE
Confidential

IMAGES
Marie-Louise Halpenny

This building is the result of an international competition in 2005 to create a new visitor centre for the UNESCO World Heritage Site of the Giant's Causeway. The scheme can be understood as two folds in the landscape: one folds up to accommodate the building, and the second folds down to house the car park. Between these two folds a ramp leads down to a coastal path, with a 1-kilometre walk to the causeway itself. This physical separation, though counter-intuitive, is deliberate: the visitor centre does not adversely impinge on the attraction it serves. The same thing has been done at Stonehenge, although there the need was greater. Here, the visitor centre is perfectly appropriate, as much a piece of geology as it is architecture.

The building appears born of its place. Two geometries play against each other and march through the scheme from the overall layout to the detailed setting-out of the paving. The irregular lines of basalt columns grow and recede into the landscape to form the building's edges. Spatially, it is quite simple: a large single space, with stepping floor plates (think tectonic ones) leading from the entrance and ticketing through to the exit for the walk (or bus) down to the causeway. The space is made from a large concrete soffit, with slices of rooflights allowing natural illumination deep into the plan, and slots between the basalt columns giving side light to the route. Back of house is hidden away and tightly planned and managed in order to meet strict area-planning constraints.

The building is environmentally sensitive in every respect. It achieves a BREEAM rating of 'Excellent' through the use of high levels of insulation and thermal mass, utilizing the landscape itself for passive solar gain and as a heat exchanger for the ground-source heat pump. This takes the form of a 1-kilometre matrix of earth pipes (long enough to reach the causeway, had that been the plan), bringing sea air to pre-cool the building in summer and preheat it in winter.

The building may be read as and reduced to the execution of a compelling diagram, but to do so would be a disservice; the reality is greater than this. It is an all-too-rare example of the clarity of a powerful original idea being developed and built with extreme care and without compromise through to successful completion.

The swooping concrete soffit lends the interior of the visitor centre a sepulchral quality.

The basalt stacks that form the walls
of the building grow and diminish in
the same way as the columns of the
causeway itself.

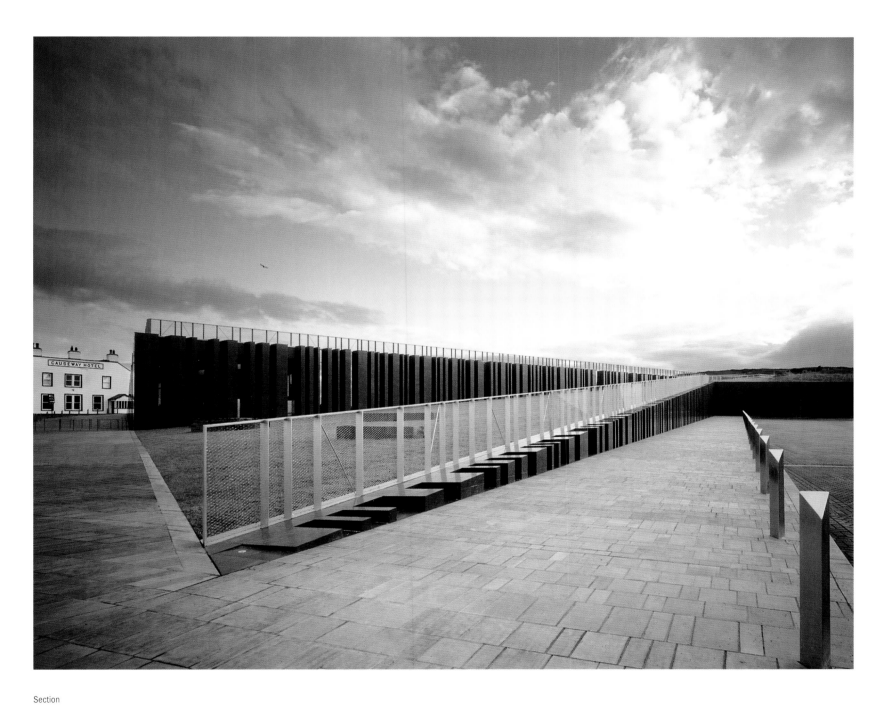

Section

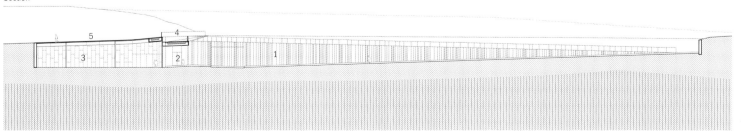

2013

NEWHALL BE
Harlow, Essex

ALISON BROOKS ARCHITECTS

Community architecture: the careful yet apparently casual grouping of the different house types creates a sense of a community that has grown over time.

Alison Brooks Architects' housing scheme for Galliford Try in Harlow, Essex, is a spirited departure from the normative design associated with suburban house-building. It is significant not just for its bold appearance, but also for its intelligent rethinking of the needs of the suburban house and the issue of how each unit relates to its neighbour.

The masterplan of eighty-four houses forms the latest phase of development on the Newhall site. Landowners Will and Jon Moen have established a reputation for responsible development based on well-considered architecture. This gave Brooks some leverage in convincing Galliford Try to move away from a standard approach and opt for something different. Equally convincing was the architects' innovation of 'terraced patio houses', which a enabled higher density of homes to be accommodated on the site. The whole is an efficient mix of new and familiar house typologies, including courtyard houses, terrace houses, a perimeter of free-standing villas, and apartment buildings that mark prominent junctions. It is united by a strong geometric and material consistency, apparently inspired by the sculptural roof forms and simple materials of traditional Essex barns.

Conventional long and narrow development plots have been rejected in favour of wider, squarer ones that allow the houses more breathing space, enabling the interiors to capture light from different directions. The architects persuaded the housing developer Galliford Try that investing in quality adds to the bottom line, but only in the long run. So by halving the size of the gardens – and creating roof terraces that in total equal the area of 'lost' land – the architects managed to get an extra six houses on to the development. Rather than directly increasing the developer's margin, this paid for such extras as full-height windows, dedicated studies and convertible roof space – things that do not feature in standard house-builders' products. The houses were then easier to sell in a difficult market.

The layout demands a more communal lifestyle than is usual on a typical suburban estate. An effort has been made to make the street an extension of the living space; balconies and studies face it, so that people working at home are not isolated in their bedrooms. The approach is refreshing and sensible. On a tight budget, this project delivers houses that are a joy to live in, designed with intelligence and imagination. This is a fine achievement in its own right. In the context of much of the UK's new house-building, it is truly exceptional.

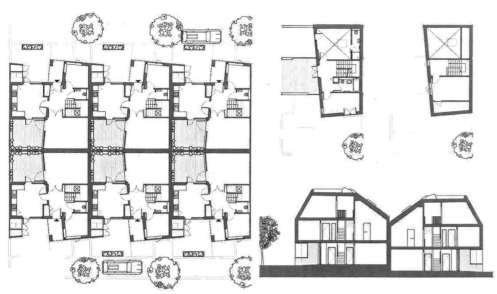

CLIENTS/CONTRACTORS
Galliford Try Partnerships; Linden
Homes Eastern

MASTERPLANNERS
Studio REAL; Alison Brooks Architects

STRUCTURAL ENGINEER
Thomasons

CONTRACT VALUE
£12 million

IMAGES
Paul Riddle – VIEW

Ground-floor plans and section of terraced patio houses

2013

PARK HILL PHASE 1
South Street, Park Hill, Sheffield

HAWKINS\BROWN WITH STUDIO EGRET WEST

It is hard now to recall the excitement once engendered by the expression 'streets in the sky'. We had never had it so good: density and community in one social mix, with milk floats passing the door six storeys up in the air. Sheffield saw the boldest of such experiments, and it was not the architecture that failed, but the maintenance of it.

This is a sensitive regeneration of a heroic Grade II*-listed building that was maligned on account of the problems associated with run-down social housing. Urban Splash, having saved Liverpool and Manchester, or at least kick-started their regeneration, has turned its attention to the other side of the Pennines. And it is to be commended for sticking with it through the thick of the recession, rather than bailing out as lesser developers would have done. Urban Splash appointed two complementary firms of architects: Hawkins\Brown and Studio Egret West, though it does rather seem as if they egged each other on.

Level 12 plan

New iridescent coloured panels give the street frontage a changing face while not challenging the original architecture. In fact, the vibrant panels borrow from the gradated and now faded pastel colours of the original brickwork, giving a Corbusian vigour to the façades. The architects have also addressed the often contradictory demands of conservation and commerce. Working with stakeholders English Heritage, they have found a balance between retaining the brutalist language while giving it a fresh translation, thus changing public perception of the building.

The original aspiration of the late 1950s blocks was to resemble an Italian hill village, and the topography was certainly right: like Rome, Sheffield is built on seven hills. But the linear blocks had degenerated into a sorry and threatening place to be. Now the completed first phase shows what a lick of paint and an otherwise surprising amount of restraint can do. While doubling the amount of glazing, the architects have retained the character of the concrete and exposed more of it inside the split-level apartments, removing some internal walls to fill the rooms with light. And to remind us of what was, other blocks remain empty and forlorn (many mid-century purists may prefer them that way). The original streets have been made safe with security measures and a metre borrowed from their generous width to add to the accommodation (so there are no more milk floats). Set-back doorways and corner windows also humanize spaces, allowing for discreet surveillance and a greater sense of ownership.

CLIENT
Urban Splash

STRUCTURAL ENGINEER
Stockley

SERVICES ENGINEER
Ashmount

LANDSCAPE CONSULTANT
Grant Associates

CONTRACTOR
Urban Splash Build

CONTRACT VALUE
Confidential

IMAGES
Daniel Hopkinson

Opposite: The blocks follow the contours of one of Sheffield's seven hills in an organic fashion.

Above and left: The architects have humanized the 'streets in the sky', extending the flats by building out into them by a metre, but with set-backs, and have softened the elevations by means of colour and additional glazing.

2013

UNIVERSITY OF LIMERICK MEDICAL SCHOOL, STUDENT HOUSING AND BUS SHELTER
Limerick, Ireland

GRAFTON ARCHITECTS

CLIENT
Plassey Campus Developments

STRUCTURAL ENGINEER
PUNCH Consulting Engineers

SERVICES ENGINEER
Don O'Malley & Partners

CONTRACTOR
P.J. Hegarty & Sons

CONTRACT VALUE
€12.1 million

IMAGES
Dennis Gilbert – VIEW

The blocks of student housing resemble villas of great gravitas, and speak of the importance of education in Ireland.

In a year when half the Stirling shortlist was designed by Irish-born architects, the Limerick scheme best demonstrates the health of architectural creativity amid the ruins of the Republic's economy. The brief was to deliver, within an existing masterplan, a building to accommodate the functions of the university's new Graduate Entry Medicine Programme, halls of residence to house 100 students, and a public open space connected to a cross-campus road and adjacent to a new pedestrian bridge (a previous RIBA Award-winner by Wilkinson Eyre) that links the North and South Campuses across the River Shannon. Grafton's ensemble, consisting of a medical school, three blocks of student housing and a bus shelter, combines with three existing neighbouring institutions to make the new public space.

The structure of the Medical School is an *in-situ* concrete frame. This framework is infilled with concrete blockwork, which is exposed internally and clad externally in local limestone. The strongly sculpted forms give a particularly civic quality to a campus that desperately needs such seriousness. Grafton Architects is a master of light, understanding how it shapes space. Here it pours in through high windows, illumining what might otherwise be sepulchral spaces. Off this atrium are teaching and study areas designed as rich theatrical spaces on an almost heroic scale. The buildings also have a generous attitude to the surrounding public space: open undercrofts provide routes through the campus, while deep thresholds make welcoming places in which to pause and gather. From joints to masterplan, every element has been carefully considered. The aspiration was to combine faculty buildings and residences in a manner that encourages overlap and contributes to the life of the public spaces at the university. The three blocks of student accommodation resemble oversized grand villas instead of the rabbit hutches that so many students have to inhabit. The canted rooflines

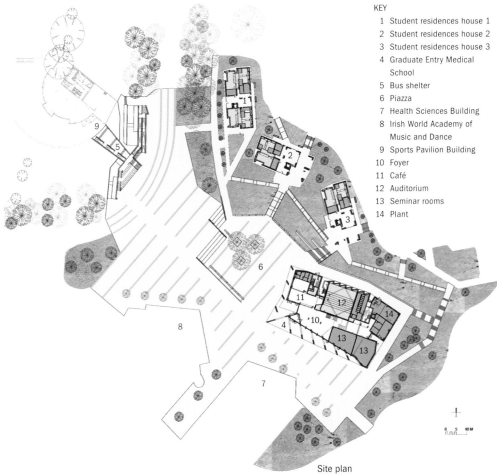

Site plan

and the deeply carved openings in the brick walls lend a sense of both quality and permanence.

This whole scheme represents remarkable value for money. The client should be shouting the fact from its elegant rooftops. And it should be praising the architects for delivering Oxbridge-quality buildings for the cost of an average supermarket: €1220 per square metre – less than £1000. Remarkable, although maybe not to be attempted at home.

Above and right: The Medical School uses the language of limestone, in contrast to the domestic red brick of the housing. Inside, the school is an essay in light and shade.

2014

WINNER

EVERYMAN THEATRE
Hope Street, Liverpool
HAWORTH TOMPKINS

SHORTLIST

LIBRARY OF BIRMINGHAM
Centenary Square, Birmingham
MECANOO

LONDON AQUATICS CENTRE
Queen Elizabeth Olympic Park, London E20
ZAHA HADID ARCHITECTS

**MANCHESTER SCHOOL OF ART,
MANCHESTER METROPOLITAN UNIVERSITY**
Cavendish Street, Manchester
FEILDEN CLEGG BRADLEY STUDIOS

**SAW SWEE HOCK STUDENT CENTRE,
LONDON SCHOOL OF ECONOMICS AND
POLITICAL SCIENCE**
Sheffield Street, London WC2
O'DONNELL + TUOMEY

THE SHARD
London Bridge Street, London SE1
RENZO PIANO BUILDING WORKSHOP

JUDGES

SPENCER DE GREY
Architect, Stirling Prize winner in 1998
and 2004, and shortlisted in 1998–2000,
2003–2005 and 2007 (chair)

STEPHEN KIERAN
Architect

M.J. LONG
Architect

SIR TIMOTHY SAINSBURY
Patron of architecture

CINDY WALTERS
Architect

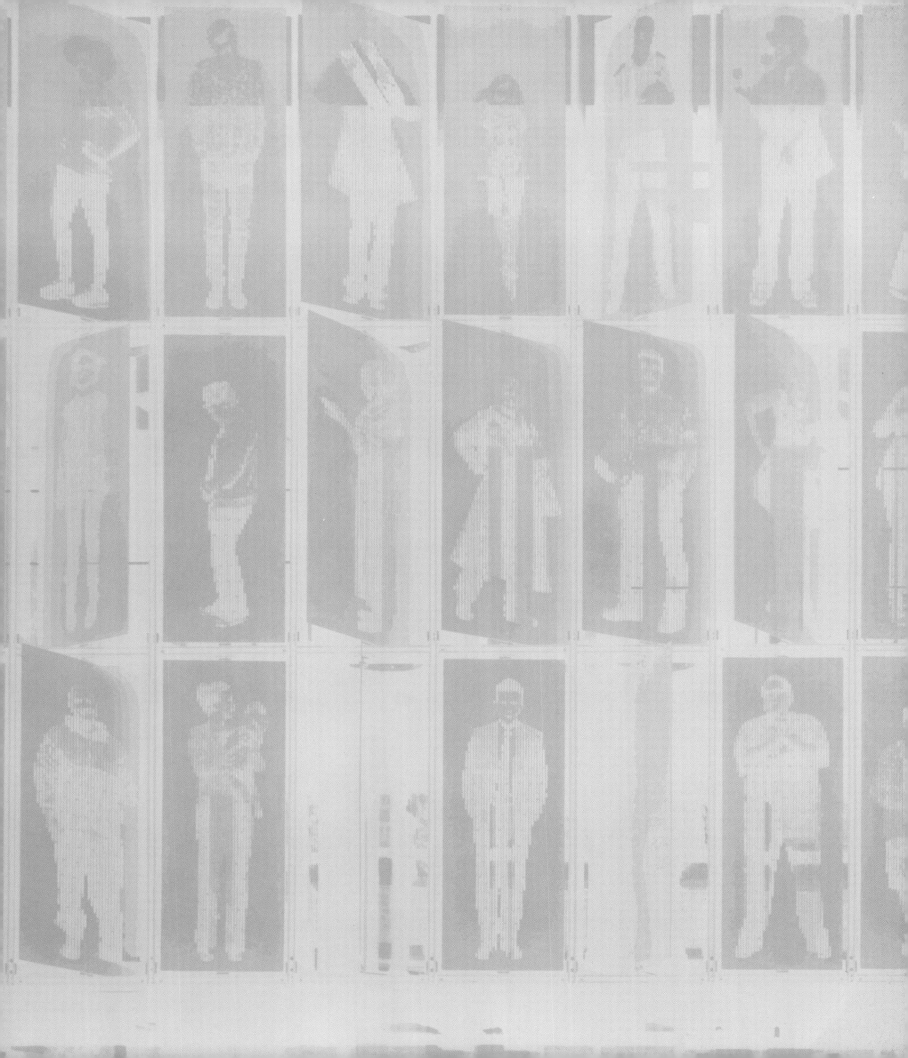

2014

EVERYMAN THEATRE
Hope Street, Liverpool

HAWORTH TOMPKINS

The new Everyman feels like a found space. It draws on the themes and ideas of Haworth Tompkins's previous theatre work at the Royal Court and the Young Vic (pp. 102–103), both in London. Here all is new-build, yet it has the ambience of an old building, in part because of the use of recycled and exposed brick in the major areas of auditorium, bars and circulation. This is a building that breathes quality in its choice of materials, its lighting and its signage. Everything has been carefully considered and the right decisions have been reached. The tour de force is the first-floor bar, a *piano nobile* stretching across the front of the building. Tucked in behind is a nook of a writers' room with the air of a gentlemen's club. The auditorium, with its burnt-orange upholstery, is a clever cross between Frank Matcham and the cosy cinema feel of the original.

The old theatre, converted from a nineteenth-century chapel on one of the city's most important streets, was among the most cherished of Liverpool's cultural assets; however, it was totally unsuited to productions and audiences in the twenty-first century. Consequently, the challenge to build a new purpose-built theatre on the site of the original was a brave but key move by the client. In selecting Haworth Tompkins, it found a partner that understood the essence of the organization and its ambitions. Over the course of nine years they worked closely together to deliver a building of outstanding quality that retains the unique values of the Everyman.

The new building includes a technically advanced and highly adaptable 400-seat theatre that exactly mirrors the shape of the original theatre, smaller performance spaces, a rehearsal room, a sumptuous green room, a public foyer, café and bar, along with supporting office and ancillary spaces. Back and front of house are turned out using identical materials and with the same attention to detail. Haworth Tompkins has created a building that instinctively

In the shadow of Frederick Gibberd's Roman Catholic cathedral, the Everyman provides Liverpool with a new piece of appropriately urban architecture, one that speaks to the city's inhabitants in a forthright language.

2014

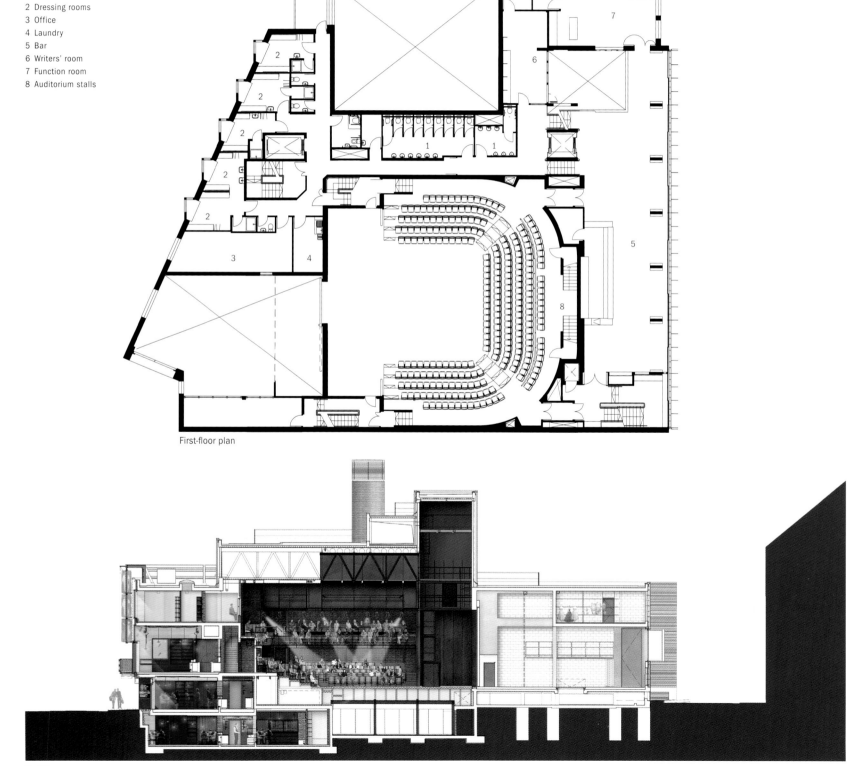

KEY
1 Toilets
2 Dressing rooms
3 Office
4 Laundry
5 Bar
6 Writers' room
7 Function room
8 Auditorium stalls

First-floor plan

Section

At the heart of the scheme is a
re-creation (using the same bricks)
of the old chapel-turned-Everyman
Theatre.

you want to reach out and touch. Its handrails, walls and exquisite purpose-built joinery are all equally tactile. The concrete is good but never precious. No single element shouts out above the others; together, they simply add to the whole, amplifying this exceptional piece of architecture.

As well as perhaps making a statement about this being a factory for play-making, the four chimneys announce the theatre's environmental credentials. A Roman section of air voids runs through the building. The strategy has outperformed all forecasts: despite a hot first summer, a windowless room with 400 people in it and all that stage lighting, leading to temperatures of 29°C, there was still no need to use the mechanical ventilation.

The most discussed – and locally loved – feature of the new Everyman is the etched-metal brise-soleil on the façade, featuring 105 full-length cut-out figures based on photographs of Liverpudlians. Anywhere else this might be seen as patronizing, but this is Liverpool, which loves to

wear its heart on its sleeve. This is a building that will age gracefully, continually enriched by the patina of daily use. It will both reassure and delight its loyal audience and those discovering this gem for the first time.

Steve Tompkins, project director, told the Stirling judges: 'Although the architecture is new, there is a duty of care, if you like, to the continuity of the place, the organization and the audience, and equally an aspiration to reinvent the Everyman so the audience will be just as inspired by it. One of the conversations that our studio has been having is, what makes good theatre space, and why do artists, audiences, directors and actors love found space and hate new buildings? That's a real challenge for architects. It's a deeply troubling paradox for those of us who spend our time inventing new buildings. We had the chance to recycle the old building and we had the space to do it, so we took the opportunity, and we recycled and reused over 90 per cent of the old Everyman Theatre. As part of that, we reused about

2014

On opening night of the new theatre, the auditorium hosted a production of *Twelfth Night*.

This is also a place where non-theatregoers can hang out, with the upper foyer situated above the bar (shown below), which sits above the bistro.

25,000 bricks from the original chapel to make the shell of the auditorium, as a box within a box of the new building.'

Gemma Bodinetz, the client and artistic director of the theatre, commented: 'The thing that is woven through it all is that word "Everyman" and what that old Everyman was. And that's not something you can transport to Stanley Dock, nor indeed can you just put that neon sign on the side of any old building without it being a cruel joke.'

The Everyman is a serious building in a serious context. Overlooked by Frederick Gibberd's Roman Catholic cathedral on its monumental mound, the theatre holds its own, appearing as if it has always been there, yet it is contemporary and stylish – very much a part of the new Liverpool.

CLIENT
The Liverpool and Merseyside Theatres Trust

STRUCTURAL ENGINEER
Alan Baxter & Associates

SERVICES ENGINEER
Waterman Building Services

CONTRACTOR
Gilbert Ash

CONTRACT VALUE
£13.3 million

IMAGES
Brian Roberts (left); Philip Vile (p. 214; p. 215; p. 217; above)

2014

CLIENT
Birmingham City Council

STRUCTURAL/SERVICES ENGINEER
Buro Happold

CONTRACTOR
Carillion

CONTRACT VALUE
£186 million

IMAGES
Harry Cock (opposite, bottom);
Mecanoo (right); Christian Richters –
VIEW (opposite, top)

The library is a box of tricks – simple boxes and drums stacked and connected with adroitness and ambition seldom seen in public architecture today.

Section

LIBRARY OF BIRMINGHAM
Centenary Square, Birmingham

MECANOO

Who said the book is dead? If the book is dead, long live the library. While other local authorities are doing the government's bidding in implementing spending cuts, saving pennies by closing libraries, albeit at the expense of our children's futures, Birmingham has invested heavily in the power of the word.

It takes good architects to give form to political will, and the City of Birmingham has appointed successive excellent firms to do so: first Rogers, whose fine design was never realized, and latterly Mecanoo, whose first major UK project this is. Playing an important role in Birmingham's Centenary Square, the new Library of Birmingham is an impressive and bold addition to the city, a truly public and civic building.

The library's intriguing section connects the internal atrium to the square outside, creating a number of levels where users can enjoy the spaces. The journey through the building reveals itself through the interlocking atrium, tying together a range of volumes and providing glimpses of natural light. From the 'Harry Potter' rotunda to the 'Willy Wonka' glass lift, not to mention the more pedestrian escalators, the library is a journey up through the building's five floors – passing through the circular reference library, which is arranged in a similar way to the old Reading Room of the British Museum – to the archives placed counter-intuitively but successfully on the upper floors. The interesting filigree screen on the elevations produces a strong sense of place and ever-changing vistas from within. Externally, the screen is the signature of this landmark, and lends grace to the otherwise box-like forms of the three stacked palazzos. It also reflects the heritage of Birmingham's Jewellery Quarter, and plays out in shadows and reflections on the library's walls and floors. The elevated, landscaped gardens on the upper floors provide not only a sanctuary in an urban location, but also breathtaking views across the city.

The library is a world-class facility for a world-class city, with formal and informal spaces for reading, relaxing and participating in the programme of events. It has become the focal point of the city's literary culture, transforming Centenary Square from an interim space into a vibrant city square. It has also changed the traditional perception of a library, making it a place where families and readers can spend a whole day learning and engaging. The John Madin brutalist predecessor library will be much missed, but its joyful replacement has already claimed its place in Brummies' hearts.

Mecanoo has created added treats, with generous terraces and the surprisingly lofty spaces of the lending library.

2014

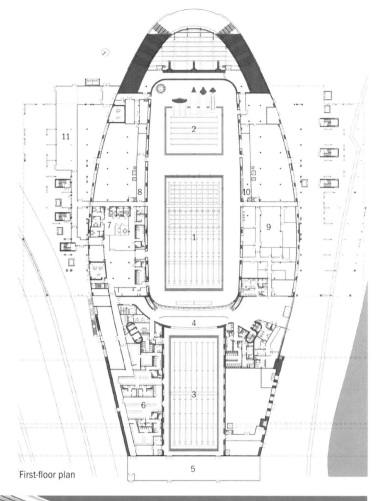

First-floor plan

SHORTLISTED

LONDON AQUATICS CENTRE
Queen Elizabeth Olympic Park, London E20

ZAHA HADID ARCHITECTS

Flexible buildings are frequently dull; compromise means that none of the functions is properly served. At the Olympic Park, Zaha Hadid Architects designed for legacy a world-class building with a distinctive curvaceous form. Then it designed the removable 'wings' that accommodated the additional seating required by spectators during the Olympic Games. It is the subsequent clipping of those wings that has allowed the building, architecturally speaking, to fly free. The concept was inspired by the fluid geometry of water in motion, creating spaces and a surrounding environment in sympathy with the river landscape of the Olympic Park. An undulating roof sweeps up from the ground like a wave folding over the building, defining the separate training and performance-cum-diving pool halls. The main hall, with its acoustically treated timber ceiling, allows for normal conversation across the screeches of delighted swimmers.

Despite the unusually stringent demand for the building to work as both an Olympic venue and, in its purer form, a public swimming pool, the resulting centre has proved successful in both scenarios. The building has three main components: a concrete podium, cast *in situ*; a wide-spanning steel roof, encased in timber louvres on its underbelly and with aluminium cladding, with standing seams, on top; between the two are glazed façades with bronze-coloured aluminium frames. There were exceptionally complex site constraints. The main pedestrian access route had to be via the new Stratford City Bridge. The solution was to have a podium encasing the main pool hall, on axis, perpendicular to the bridge, off which is the entrance, with the training pool slotted under the bridge within the podium.

The building's sustainability credentials are exemplary; it achieved a BREEAM Innovation Credit for its unusual use of concrete mixes, far exceeding the targets of the Olympic Delivery Authority. The main pool is naturally lit. Mechanical systems have adaptable controls for maximum efficiencies in use, and the building is connected to the district heating system. Potable water demands were reduced by more than 40 per cent. Rainwater harvesting provides irrigation for the green wall at the southern end of the building. Overall, this is a very beautiful scheme; it is sensual in its form, with a generosity of space. It works very practically and is well built, with exceptionally high-quality finishes. Its pure and powerful form is conceptually flawless, and undoubtedly it will be a favourite venue of Londoners for generations to come.

Opposite and below: As in the case of all good campuses, the buildings of London's Olympic Park speak to one another. Here, the voluminous curves of the Aquatics Centre echo those of the Velodrome, even if the echoes are fortuitous.

Left: The roof is expressed internally, allowing the made-for-TV drama to continue throughout the scheme.

CLIENTS
London Organising Committee of the Olympic and Paralympic Games; Olympic Delivery Authority

STRUCTURAL/SERVICES ENGINEER
Arup

CONTRACTOR
Balfour Beatty

CONTRACT VALUE
Confidential

IMAGES
Hufton + Crow – VIEW

2014

MANCHESTER SCHOOL OF ART, MANCHESTER METROPOLITAN UNIVERSITY
Cavendish Street, Manchester

FEILDEN CLEGG BRADLEY STUDIOS

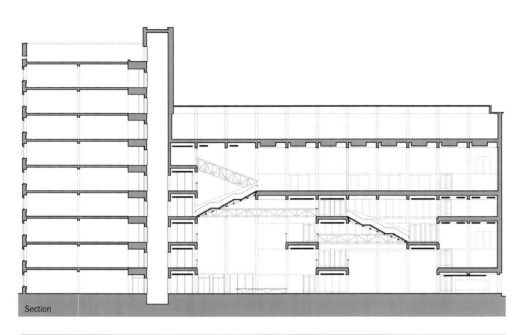

Section

It feels as if you are entering a metropolitan art gallery rather than a university department. This is an atrium with real purpose, providing the public (who are allowed in thus far) and students with glimpses of works of art and their making. Different disciplines can see what their confrères are up to, and are encouraged to mix and collaborate: graphic arts with fine arts, architecture with fashion, photography with jewellery.

This major refurbishment of the 1960s tower and new extension to the Manchester School of Art has been executed with great skill by Feilden Clegg Bradley Studios. Design excellence has been coupled with the brief of a visionary client to break down the traditional art and design units, encouraging staff and students across disciplines to work together and explore the common ground between their subjects. Art school education should be about helping students to think in a non-linear way, to be receptive to a variety of creative approaches. Fittingly, FCBS has thought about this building in a non-linear, vertical way. The scheme will influence the design of all art schools and many other university buildings for years to come.

The welcoming 'vertical gallery' space is open to all, enabling students and visitors to perambulate up gently rising flying staircases. Behind the vertical element sits the 'design shed', where open studios, workshops and teaching areas provide a wide range of spaces for learning.

The discreet security systems allow students to access studios without the need for endless turnstiles, which often

CLIENT
Manchester Metropolitan University

STRUCTURAL/SERVICES ENGINEER
Arup

CONTRACTOR
Morgan Sindall

CONTRACT VALUE
£23.6 million

IMAGES
Hufton + Crow − VIEW

plague such buildings. Large custom-made hangar doors enable the 'shed' to open up to the public vertical space for exhibitions or other events. These doors are among a number of innovative design solutions that have been cleverly incorporated throughout the scheme.

The client, Professor John Brooks, Vice Chancellor of the university, demonstrated a refreshing refusal either to submit to the notion of art for art's sake or to accept that a decent

provision for the arts is a luxury we cannot afford in the current economic climate. This building is a catalyst for the exploration of design and creativity. As the school prospectus states, 'Manchester School of Art believes an art school is more than just a place. It is a bridge between the acceptable and the possible, between what is and what if.' Those words could well have been describing the then unbuilt Feilden Clegg Bradley School of Art.

Opposite: The bold section lifts this economical building into the realm of the special, encouraging interaction and interdisciplinary working.

Above: A factory for art: there is a tough plainness to the exterior that announces that this scheme is less about art for art's sake, more about art for all's sake.

2014

**SAW SWEE HOCK STUDENT CENTRE, LONDON
SCHOOL OF ECONOMICS AND POLITICAL SCIENCE**
Sheffield Street, London WC2

O'DONNELL + TUOMEY

Opposite: This is Lego for grown-ups, but the imagination required in designing such complex forms, with not a single cut brick, is beyond that of any child – and of most architects.

Below: This is a place of stairs; here, a peel of concrete leads down to the basement performance space.

In the midst of a complex medieval London street pattern, O'Donnell + Tuomey has woven a little of its magic. This remarkable project is an object lesson in mobilizing the limitations of a site into a startlingly original building that makes a massive contribution to the townscape. The architects started by taking the geometry of tight angles as the definition of a solid, out of which they gouged cuts and cracks that give light and form. Every angled facet responds to the rights of lights of its neighbours. The momentum is generated in the surrounding streets and drawn into a spiral that rises through the whole height of the structure as a continuous internal street, taking the form of a generous stair that clambers its way around the core. Outer walls slope and twist, and floors take up complex non-orthogonal shapes, yet all the accommodation generated seems to be natural, functional and hugely enjoyable to use.

The bold red-brick tower is made of not just any brick: there are 46 'standard' special bricks used to make non-standard corners and 127 one-off special bricks. The remaining bricks – out of a total of 175,000 – are regular, but there is not a single cut brick. This has been achieved by means of walls that slope, become perforated screens that offer shading and have angles that vary in every direction, all suggesting a very considerable imaginative control. The latticing lets in more light, lending the scheme a Kahnian air. The windows use jatoba, a self-finished hardwood from Brazil, and have a complexity of their own whereby many verticals are gathered together next to larger panes, the verticals indicating opening windows. The spiral plan functions as a continuous social space with a natural tendency to encourage interaction between students and staff. At the top and bottom of the system are two more conventional spiral staircases, one to the basement and the other to the highest part of the diminishing plan. In the basement, there is a large, double-height club and bar space lit by borrowed daylight from street level. The use of daylight and natural ventilation, among many other environmental initiatives, has resulted in a BREEAM rating of 'Outstanding'.

O'Donnell + Tuomey's work is always recognizable but ever-developing, and full of architectural references: not just Louis Kahn, but also James Stirling and the Russian Constructivists. The practice absorbs such references and makes buildings that are all its own – and are much admired by their clients and those who use them.

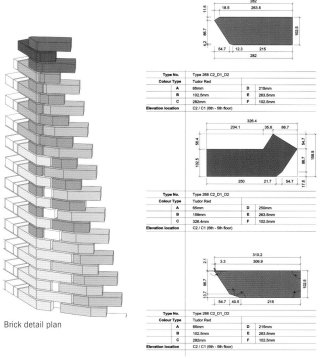

Brick detail plan

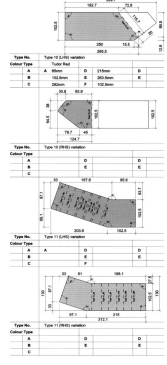

Type No.	Type 268 C2_D1_D2		
Colour Type	Tudor Red		
A	65mm	D	215mm
B	102.5mm	E	263.5mm
C	282mm	F	102.5mm
Elevation location	C2 / C1 (6th - 5th floor)		

Type No.	Type 268 C2_D1_D2		
Colour Type	Tudor Red		
A	65mm	D	250mm
B	159mm	E	263.5mm
C	326.4mm	F	102.5mm
Elevation location	C2 / C1 (6th - 5th floor)		

Type No.	Type 266 C2_D1_D2		
Colour Type	Tudor Red		
A	65mm	D	215mm
B	102.5mm	E	263.5mm
C	282mm	F	102.5mm
Elevation location	C2 / C1 (6th - 5th floor)		

Type No.	Type 10 (LHS) variation			
Colour Type	Tudor Red			
A	A	65mm	D	215mm	D
B		102.5mm	E	263.5mm	E
C		282mm	F	102.5mm	

Type No.	Type 10 (RHS) variation		
Colour Type			
A		D	D
B		E	E
C			

Type No.	Type 11 (LHS) variation		
Colour Type			
A	A	D	D
B		E	E
C		F	

Type No.	Type 11 (RHS) variation		
Colour Type			
A		D	D
B		E	E
C			

CLIENT
London School of Economics and Political Science

STRUCTURAL ENGINEER
Horgan Lynch

SERVICES ENGINEER
BDSP Partnership

CONTRACTOR
Osborne

CONTRACT VALUE
£24.12 million

IMAGES
Dennis Gilbert – VIEW

SHORTLISTED

THE SHARD
London Bridge Street, London SE1

RENZO PIANO BUILDING WORKSHOP

CLIENT
London Bridge Quarter

STRUCTURAL ENGINEER
WSP Cantor Seinuk

SERVICES ENGINEER
Arup

CONTRACTOR
Mace

CONTRACT VALUE
Confidential

IMAGES
Michel Denancé

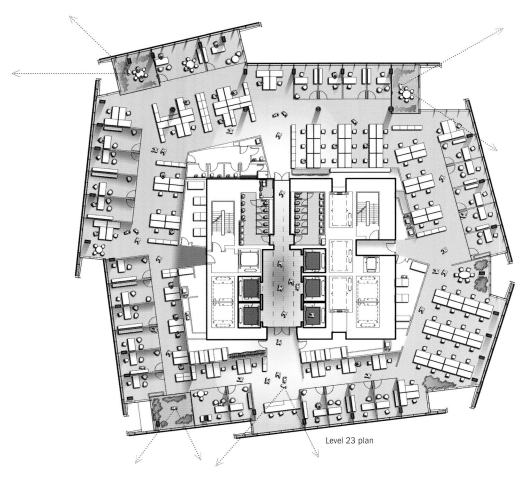

Level 23 plan

It is a rare achievement to make a tower on such a tight site a thing of beauty. The architects have added immeasurably to the immediate environs and to London as a whole. The Shard makes people talk about architecture, which can only be a good thing. But there is much for architects to admire, too: the way the building meets the split ground level while expressing its structure; the way one keeps seeing the structure from the inside of the building; and the way the structure shines when it frames the views from the uppermost public platforms.

There cannot be a more compressed or a more exemplary model for city intensification than this tower: some 111,500 square metres of accommodation built on a tiny parcel of land next to one of London's transport hubs. It has six uses, each occupying multiple floors: health clinic, offices, restaurants, hotel, residential apartments and public viewing gallery – a genuine vertical village. All this touches the ground effortlessly, with offices and viewing gallery – the high-volume uses – approached directly from a podium facing London Bridge station, and the rest from street level on the opposite side.

The Shard's three great virtues are all related to its external appearance. First, the floor-plate depths are graded according to the uses they contain (offices require deeper floor plates than hotels and apartments), so that the building tapers elegantly. Moreover, this elegance is always present,

The Shard has become as emblematic of London in the second decade of this century as the Gherkin was in the first.

The Shard has become as emblematic of London in the second decade of this century as the Gherkin was in the first.

no matter how much of the overall form is hidden by other buildings. Secondly, with the perimeter modelled as eight distinct 'shards', the scale of the building is fragmented and the light reflected in interesting ways – not least by dint of the way in which the angled glass reflects the ever-changing sky, rather than the static cityscape, lending a sense of lightness few other towers can claim. Thirdly, understanding that there are many days when the London skyline reads only as a depressing grey silhouette, the architects have left a substantial part at the top open, not unlike the lattice form of many Germanic Gothic cathedral spires, adding further to the lightness even in such conditions. If one looks through the gap between Big Ben and Portcullis House – a view subject to challenge in a recent public inquiry – the Shard appears next to the spires of the Palace of Westminster with the inevitability of an established and historic part of London's skyline.

2015

WINNER

BURNTWOOD SCHOOL
Burntwood Lane, London SW17
ALLFORD HALL MONAGHAN MORRIS

SHORTLIST

DARBISHIRE PLACE
John Fisher Street, London E1
NÍALL McLAUGHLIN ARCHITECTS

**MAGGIE'S LANARKSHIRE,
MONKLANDS HOSPITAL**
Airdrie, North Lanarkshire
REIACH AND HALL ARCHITECTS

NEO BANKSIDE
Holland Street, London SE1
**ROGERS STIRK HARBOUR + PARTNERS
WITH JOHN ROBERTSON ARCHITECTS**

UNIVERSITY OF GREENWICH
Stockwell Street, London SE10
HENEGHAN PENG ARCHITECTS

**THE WHITWORTH,
THE UNIVERSITY OF MANCHESTER**
Oxford Road, Manchester
MUMA

JUDGES

JANE DUNCAN
RIBA President (chair)

PETER CLEGG
Architect, Stirling Prize winner in 2008 and
shortlisted in 2014

RORY OLCAYTO
Editor of *The Architects' Journal*

DAME THERESA SACKLER
Philanthropist and Trustee of the Sackler
Foundation and the Sackler Trust

STEVE TOMPKINS
Architect, Stirling Prize winner in 2014 and
shortlisted in 2007

2015

BURNTWOOD SCHOOL
Burntwood Lane, London SW17

ALLFORD HALL MONAGHAN MORRIS

Burntwood School owes its very existence to the initiative of a handful of pupils who, when they heard about the scrapping of the Building Schools for the Future (BSF) programme and with it their planned new school, took it upon themselves to go to Westminster to lobby the Education Secretary, Michael Gove, in person. Their strategy worked: Burntwood was one of the few schools to survive the savage cull.

This is a truly collaborative project in which mature architects with a deep understanding and experience of what makes for a good school, working with landscapers who believe that a light touch can transform an existing landscape, and a graphic artist whose work has long made wayfinding an art form in AHHM projects, have produced one last hurrah for BSF. And, lest we forget, BSF may have been based on a wasteful methodology, but it did have at its heart a desire to improve the fabric and learning environments of UK schools.

Burntwood is a high-achieving school with 1800 pupils, almost all girls, in a relatively poor part of south London. It reminds us of an earlier time when such aspirations were the norm: the 1950s and early 1960s, when the LCC and GLC programmes led by Leslie Martin were providing London with light-filled, beautifully organized schools. Here at Burntwood two fine Martin-designed buildings have informed the new architecture, notwithstanding that one, the swimming pool, was rudely over-clad in the 1980s. It is the relationship between the new concrete buildings and the older ones that adds a sense of architectural history and depth to the whole site – that, and a landscape that has had fifty years to mature.

These are buildings of great force. A modular precast concrete cladding, made using eight different moulds, with canted edges and different-sized glazing panels, is playfully arranged on a rigid grid, creating surprising interior spaces. This grid stops short of the corners, effectively dissolving them and softening the building into the landscape, which is a carefully orchestrated sequence of distinct new gardens.

The deeply moulded panels give precast concrete a good name, even among architects who tend to sneer at anything but the poured variety.

2015

KEY

1 Arts & Technology
2 Communications
3 Maths & Science
4 Existing pool building
5 Four-court sports hall
6 Existing assembly hall
7 Business Skills centre
8 Performing Arts/Dining
9 Main pedestrian entrance
10 Service road
11 Secondary pupil entrance
12 Staff/Deliveries
13 Staff parking
14 Multi-use games area (MUGA)
15 Sports fields

Site plan

Sections

Arts & Technology   Business Skills/Main entrance   Parking

Communications   Spine   Performing Arts/Dining   Parking

Business Skills   Communications   Maths & Science

The rooms are gracious and full of light, particularly the double- and triple-height spaces. Internal corridors all end in well-framed views. Overall, Burntwood has the collegiate atmosphere of a university campus: perhaps this is due to all the pale, finely detailed concrete; or perhaps it's the elegant covered walkway that links the principal buildings, drawing together the disparate styles and ages of the architecture. The basic module, comprising alternated precast panels, is used creatively to produce blocks of different character for different purposes. Some panels are even turned through 90 degrees to add to the interest. The old school may have had a number of distinguished buildings, but it had no street presence; the new school does, thanks to a grand double-height cut through one of the new blocks, which exposes the campus to the world and provides a vehicle for the AHMM trademark super-graphics by Morag Myerscough – here faience made of printed tiles, elsewhere murals hand-painted by the artist herself. The grand gesture of the entrance affords a great sense of arrival and an immediate impression of quality, openness, confidence and solidity.

Speaking to the Stirling judges, Paul Monaghan, the project director, said: 'It's a very simple grid, but we needed to have different-sized rooms behind, so we slid the composition to allow variety and rooms of different sizes, be they 3, 5 or 9 metres wide. The other thing about the sliding composition is that you always look out into landscape rather than on to a building, which is great because all the other schools we've done in London look on to a motorway.'

AHMM has produced grown-up buildings for Burntwood School. Instead of pandering to the pupils, the scheme makes them raise their game. This is education architecture as it should be. For the judges, Burntwood School was a clear winner. It was the most accomplished of the six shortlisted buildings because it demonstrates the full range of the skills

With its pale concrete and its sequence of landscaped gardens, Burntwood has the air of an Ivy League campus.

Right: Morag Myerscough's tiles provide strong markers for each building entrance, particularly here at the street entrance.

Below: The sports hall uses a different language, one that mediates between the precast concrete and the lightness of Leslie Martin's architecture.

Opposite: The library features the new school emblem, developed by Morag Myerscough in collaboration with the pupils.

that architects can offer to society. It encompasses great contemporary design and clever reuse of existing buildings, as well as superb integration of artwork, landscaping and engineering. It is a genuine collaborative project. There was a wonderful working relationship between the head teacher and the architect: a true partnership of equals.

Burntwood is technically sophisticated in its use of prefabrication, in its low-energy strategy and in the fact that there was minimal disruption to teachers and pupils during construction. It even has its own high street: a covered walkway formed from off-the-peg bus shelters. Furthermore, the sculptural quality of the finely modelled concrete façades and the lush campus setting enhance the sense of place. Burntwood sets a standard in school design that every child in Britain deserves. It is the culmination of years of creative toil by Allford Hall Monaghan Morris in designing schools up and down the country. This is the firm's masterpiece.

CLIENT
Wandsworth Council

STRUCTURAL ENGINEER
Buro Happold

SERVICES ENGINEER
Mott MacDonald

LANDSCAPE ARCHITECT
Kinnear Landscape Architects

GRAPHICS
Studio Myerscough

CONTRACTOR
Lendlease

CONTRACT VALUE
£40.9 million

IMAGES
Rob Parrish (p. 233 bottom); Timothy Soar (p. 232; p. 233 top; p. 235; above; right; opposite)

2015

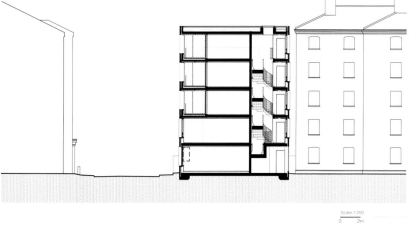

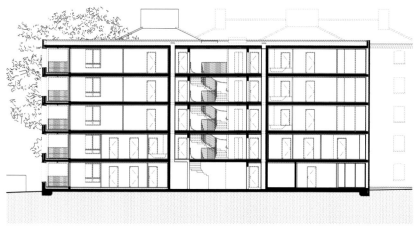

Sections

Scale 1:200
0   2m   8m

DARBISHIRE PLACE
John Fisher Street, London E1

NÍALL McLAUGHLIN ARCHITECTS

Peabody has a fine tradition of providing social housing for Londoners and appointing the best architects to help it to do so. Under the leadership of Dickon Robinson in the 1990s and the first decade of the new century, it upgraded and added to its ageing stock with excellent new developments (earning it an RIBA Client of the Year Award), but none was so exquisitely done as Níall McLaughlin's work in east London. This is a brilliant piece of urban design. The dignified new building, with its refined proportions and details, replaces a well-detailed and proportioned Peabody mansion block destroyed by a V-2 bomb during the Second World War, along with another block, the footprint of which now provides a garden at the heart of the newly completed courtyard, which is still graced by the remaining three Edwardian blocks.

A casual comparison of the old and new elevations reveals the subtlety of the new architecture. The use of materials and form means that the new building complements its neighbours without mimicking them. It represents a reinvention of the deep reveal: the employment of slightly projecting precast reveals to the windows and balconies gives an unusual depth and a delicate beauty to the modelling of the façades.

Internally, the plan naturally invites you to use the stair – and what a stair. The graceful curves, the elegant swooping handrail, the abundance of top light; all must make the residents feel like a million dollars, like stars on an ocean liner. All but the smallest flats are dual aspect. The plan also allows each flat a vestibule off the landing, an enclosed space that residents can fill with plants or the overflow from their flats; it doesn't matter, because it is theirs. The balconies likewise: each home has a generous, deep balcony from which residents can watch children play in the square.

The building oozes care. For example, the architects first chose a grey brick to match the soot-stained Victorian London brick. Peabody then decided to clean the blocks, revealing glowing cream façades. In the nick of time, the architects were able to change their order to a pale honey colour, which gives the work so much more character. Darbishire Place was delivered through design and build, but shows that the quality of the architecture and the continued involvement of the architect are more important to the success of a project than the means of its delivery. This is a proper use of an architect's skills, and makes the ordinary exceptional.

Opposite and above: As in the case of most schemes by Níall McLaughlin, apparent simplicity masks subtlety – here, a tapering plan that draws you into the square.

Left: Inside, too, careful thought can compensate for a lack of budget, as with this delightful stairwell.

CLIENT
Peabody

STRUCTURAL ENGINEER
Ellis & Moore

SERVICES ENGINEER
Nifes

CONTRACTOR
Sandwood Design and Build

CONTRACT VALUE
£23 million

IMAGES
Níall McLaughlin

2015

MAGGIE'S LANARKSHIRE, MONKLANDS HOSPITAL
Airdrie, North Lanarkshire

REIACH AND HALL ARCHITECTS

10m

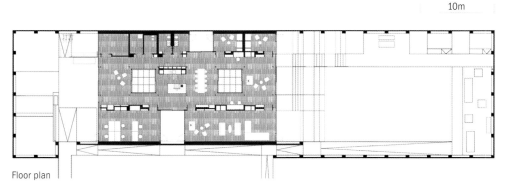

Floor plan

This new Maggie's Centre is on the old Airdrie House estate, which was enclosed by a belt of lime trees, some of which still survive. More than almost any other firm, Reiach and Hall, with its award-winning health-care experience, is ideally placed to build the bridge between the impersonality of cancer care in large hospitals and the niche-architectural approach of the womb-like Maggie's Centres, which give the recipients of terrible news hope where there is some and comfort when there is seemingly none, and provide them with the tools to go back into the world and carry on fighting.

So these architects were the perfect candidates to solve the problem: how to make something that is of the world and yet gives shelter from it; that turns its back, but does not close its eyes. The answer lies in a new surrounding perforate wall of handmade Danish brick, which recaptures some sense of paradise (the term derives from the Persian

word for 'walled enclosure') by offering a degree of separation from the nearby hospital grounds, yet prevents total disconnection between the inside and the outside.

The wall conceals a modest, low building that gathers a sequence of domestic-scaled spaces. Thus it affords a kind of passive security without blanking out the well-meaning passer-by. Visitors enter a quiet arrival court, defined by the low brick walls and two lime trees. The act of entering is an almost insurmountable step for some, an acknowledgement of what they may have long denied. But the courtyard helps: it is a place where they can linger and maybe leave. Nothing lost; they can try again. If they do come in, at once a sense of dignity and calm is encountered. A linear rill, derived from a spring, animates the space with the sound of running water. The house is as much a modest church, with a nave for the more public functions (meeting, greeting and the hearth – the Maggie's table, around which tea and mutual support are shared), as it is a home and a health building. Two unroofed courts catch sunlight, creating sheltered 'sitooteries' (a Scottish gazebo) and reflecting back a warm hearth-light via perforated stainless-steel panels. After dark, the whole building reasserts itself, giving off light instead of drawing it in. Then there are discreet 'chapels' off the side aisles: four walls and a door for more private moments.

This is a truly memorable addition to a noble tradition of specialist health buildings.

Opposite and below: Neil Gillespie of Reiach and Hall believes that people should not be denied good architecture on account of poor health or lack of income. This is perhaps one of the best-designed Maggie's Centres, in one of the poorest areas.

Left: Likewise, this is an aspirational interior worthy of any glossy design magazine or TV homes programme.

CLIENT
Maggie's

STRUCTURAL ENGINEER
Sinclair Knight Merz

SERVICES ENGINEER
K.J. Tait Engineers

LANDSCAPE ARCHITECT
Rankinfraser Landscape Architecture

CONTRACTOR
John Dennis

CONTRACT VALUE
£1.8 million

IMAGES
David Grandorge

2015

NEO BANKSIDE
Holland Street, London SE1

ROGERS STIRK HARBOUR + PARTNERS
WITH JOHN ROBERTSON ARCHITECTS

CLIENT
GC Bankside (joint venture between Native Land and Grosvenor)

STRUCTURAL ENGINEER
Waterman Group

SERVICES ENGINEER
Hoare Lea

LANDSCAPE ARCHITECT
Gillespies

CONTRACTOR
Carillion

CONTRACT VALUE
£132 million

IMAGES
Nick Guttridge (opposite, bottom); Edmund Sumner – VIEW (right; opposite, top)

NEO Bankside is seductive architecture. On a pocket of land between some single-storey almshouses and the multiple monoliths that are Tate Modern, the developers have squeezed in a group of exquisite towers and some of the best new landscaping in London. The site has history: there was to have been a single tower that was struggling to fulfil the dual role of social and private housing. The new architects designed the social housing to be on-site, but with the agreement of Southwark Council it has been redistributed throughout the borough, and almost all of it has already been delivered. A piece of land was donated by the developers for public use, to be managed by Tate as part of the planning agreement. The small-footprint private towers sit in a public garden – open until 8pm, at least – with people invited in to use the shops and cafés or just to sit and admire the luscious planting. Overall, the scheme contributes to a debate about urban design and building form, and is a well-mannered example of structurally expressive architecture.

Project-directed by partner Graham Stirk, an architect with a watchmaker's precision, this is a tour de force in its achievement of density, in its use of economical prefabricated elements and in its intricate weaving of public and private space. The form and positioning of the blocks, with their counter-intuitively chamfered corners, have resulted in very few pinch points and little overlooking, allowing 360-degree views out. On account of the exoskeletal structure and the nearly detached lift towers, the floor plates have been freed up, making the scheme more market-responsive.

The articulation of the buildings, the expressed diagrid structure (argued for by the engineers; it was to have been hidden), and the quality of the glazing systems and the external lifts make the scale feel almost cute. This is also due to the single-glazed large triangular winter gardens that dematerialize the ends of the blocks, and the triple-height structural module that reduces their perceived height. The buildings retain a human scale at ground level thanks to their rich detailing and landscaped entrance gardens. This is high-quality housing you would be unlikely to see in any other inner city worldwide – and it is ungated. Overall, the scheme has a scale and a richness that are appropriate to the lead practice and to this important part of London. Not since Alison and Peter Smithson completed the Economist Buildings in the 1960s has London been gifted an assemblage of towers of such panache.

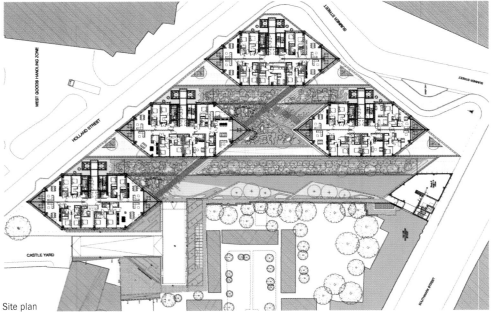

Site plan

At NEO Bankside, the Rogers aesthetic is applied to housing more successfully than ever before, most spectacularly in the penthouses (below).

2015

UNIVERSITY OF GREENWICH
Stockwell Street, London SE10

HENEGHAN PENG ARCHITECTS

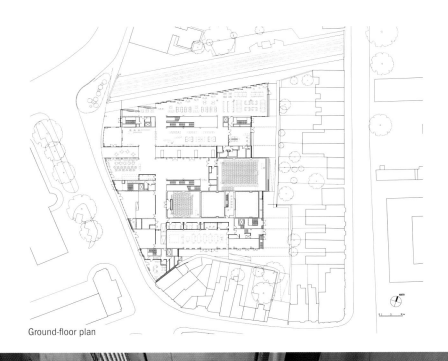

Ground-floor plan

Located in the UNESCO World Heritage Site at Maritime Greenwich and sited opposite Nicholas Hawksmoor's church of St Alfege, this building houses the main university library and the departments of Architecture, Landscape and Arts. It is a startling scheme to set down in Greenwich. Most new building in such a context is too concerned with looking over its shoulder to achieve real architecture, so it is a considerable feat to create something other than just a piece of urban knitting. This is a project that will inspire future generations of architects and also – on account of the delightful experimental rooftop allotments – landscape architects. The scheme steps down to the rear, providing generous terraces where the landscapers can experiment with a wide variety of layouts and species.

Conceptually strong in urban-design terms, the project relates well to the street in its materiality and massing. The building is broken down in both plan and section into various smaller elements separated by courtyards and staircases, and articulated at street level as a series of retail units. The plan follows a clear diagram, with its parallel fingers of accommodation separated by courtyards that extend to break up the long street-facing elevation. Externally, the forms are well articulated, giving depth and interest, with fenestration carefully considered to take advantage of key views, vistas and reflections, particularly on the long side elevation facing the railway. The building benefits from clear vertical circulation, and the acoustics are remarkably good.

In the Department of Architecture, a triple-height central crit-and-display space is visible from many levels and connects to the main stair, becoming a focal point for all the internal spaces. The graphic qualities of the diagonal form of the dark-clad linking staircase provide orientation sign-posting. Generous ceiling heights make the building light and airy to use, and allow the exposed services to sit comfortably on the polished-concrete soffits. All interiors are high quality. The architects have created cool educational spaces that can evolve over time. The lecture theatres, mostly situated underground, make up for their lack of light with a sumptuousness of materials and detailing. A nicely done gallery addresses the street, inviting the public in, as do the shop and café. This is a very public university building.

Opposite: The dramatic stair is more than the principal means of circulation; it is an art object in its own right.

Above and right: Along with Heneghan Peng, the planners are to be congratulated for the way in which these carefully modulated buildings befit a World Heritage Site.

CLIENT
University of Greenwich

STRUCTURAL ENGINEER
Alan Baxter & Associates

SERVICES ENGINEER
Hoare Lea

CONTRACTOR
Osborne

CONTRACT VALUE
£38.9 million

IMAGES
Hufton + Crow – VIEW

THE WHITWORTH,
THE UNIVERSITY OF MANCHESTER
Oxford Road, Manchester

MUMA

CLIENTS
The University of Manchester Estates;
The Whitworth

STRUCTURAL ENGINEER
Ramboll UK

SERVICES ENGINEER
Buro Happold

CONTRACTORS
ISG; Manchester & Cheshire
Construction

CONTRACT VALUE
Confidential

IMAGES
Alan Williams

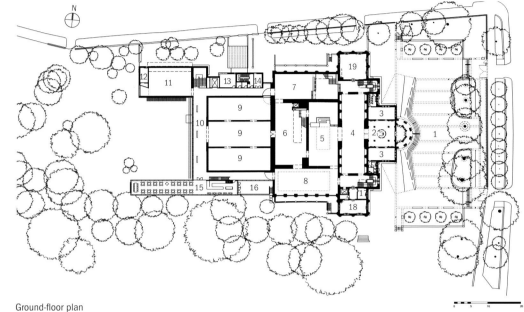

KEY
1 Carriageway/Car-parking
2 Entrance hall/Café
3 Café
4 Kitchen
5 Shop
6 Darbishire Hall – Textile Gallery
7 Gulbenkian Gallery
8 Pilkington Gallery
9 North Gallery
10 South Gallery
11 Exhibition galleries
12 Lecture theatre
13 Store
14 Worthington Room
15 Director's office
16 General office
17 Office
18 Staffroom

Ground-floor plan

A project for all seasons, where art, nature and architecture combine: this could be the eulogy to a building that is neither high-key nor overtly fashionable; rather, it is reminiscent of Alvar Aalto's designs of the 1950s. This sublime addition to the already extended nineteenth-century Whitworth Art Gallery on the edge of Whitworth Park in Manchester builds on John Bickerdike's 1960s work in a way that, as one first enters the building, seems subtle in the extreme, but then gradually builds outwards in a sympathetic but entirely original fashion. Bickerdike's galleries were made for art, not people. The worst additions from the 1960s, such as suspended ceilings, have been stripped out and earlier spatial relationships reinstated. The gallery now embraces the park it had previously turned its back on, with an elegant two-storey glazed promenade that wraps round the old blind gables. The matching cantilevered café is both a pavilion in the park and a place from which to look back into the galleries. The structural stainless-steel mullions of the new rear elevation and the café both dissolve and reflect. The café melts into the park, becoming more of a glade than a building.

The brief called for a 10 per cent reduction in the carbon footprint of the gallery despite there being an increase in its physical footprint. The scheme also revises the basis of the environmental standards for exhibiting art, with old and new galleries being sufficiently flexible to be black-box or allow in daylight. The environmental strategy is equally inventive, taking a passive-first approach that has been delivered unobtrusively, with no exposed services whatsoever – a curator's delight.

The new building has in fact doubled the public area of the gallery while increasing the overall square metreage by just a third. This has been achieved by excavating an elegant new basement collections space with well-appointed study areas. This work has in turn unlocked a spectacular grand hall, which, with its suspended ceiling and Victorian decor, was the Whitworth's big secret. Instead of housing the collections, as planned by the university, it is now a lecture hall, education space and so much more. Its exposed timber trusses and revitalized grandeur are symbolic of the way in which the architects have brought a great old institution back to life. This is not simply a conversion or adaptation of the existing structure; the new architecture emerges quite seamlessly as an integral yet individualistic part of the whole assembly.

SPONSORS

The author and publisher wish to thank and congratulate all the architects, both winners and shortlisted practices, as well as their teams of consultants and contractors, on their success in the RIBA Stirling Prize over the last twenty years.

In particular, we wish to thank the following architects for their generous financial support towards the making of this book:

FOSTER + PARTNERS
Winner with the American Air Museum in Britain, Duxford, in 1998 and 30 St Mary Axe, London, in 2004;

WILKINSON EYRE ARCHITECTS
Winner with the Magna Science Adventure Centre, Rotherham, in 2001 and the Gateshead Millennium Bridge in 2002;

EMBT
Winner (with RMJM) with the Scottish Parliament, Edinburgh, in 2005;

ROGERS STIRK HARBOUR + PARTNERS
Winner (as Richard Rogers Partnership, with Estudio Lamela) with the New Area Terminal, Barajas Airport, Madrid, in 2006 and (as RSHP) with Maggie's London in 2009;

DAVID CHIPPERFIELD ARCHITECTS
Winner with the Museum of Modern Literature, Marbach am Neckar, in 2007;

FEILDEN CLEGG BRADLEY STUDIOS, MACCREANOR LAVINGTON, ALISON BROOKS ARCHITECTS AND GRANT ASSOCIATES
Winners with Accordia, Cambridge, in 2008;

ZAHA HADID ARCHITECTS
Winner with MAXXI, Rome, in 2010 and the Evelyn Grace Academy, London, in 2011;

STANTON WILLIAMS
Winner with the Sainsbury Laboratory, Cambridge, in 2012;

WITHERFORD WATSON MANN ARCHITECTS
Winner with Astley Castle, Warwickshire, in 2013;

HAWORTH TOMPKINS
Winner with the Everyman Theatre, Liverpool, in 2014;

ALLFORD HALL MONAGHAN MORRIS
Winner with Burntwood School, London, in 2015.

Finally, we would like to thank the sponsors who have so generously supported the prize over the years:

The Sunday Times

RIBA Journal

The Architects' Journal
(in particular, Paul Finch for his unstinting support)

Benchmark

Brockton

Almacantar

INDEX

ABOUT THE AUTHORS

TONY CHAPMAN was Head of Awards at the Royal Institute of British Architects from 1998 to 2016. In 2011 he was made an Honorary Fellow of the RIBA in recognition of not only his contribution to its awards programme but also his work as a writer and film-maker. In a previous role as a BBC TV producer, he made a number of documentaries about architecture, including the modernists' riposte to the Prince of Wales's *Vision of Britain*. He is author of a dozen books about architecture, including *The Stirling Prize: Ten Years of Architecture and Innovation* (published by Merrell in 2006) and a children's book. He is currently writing a book with the architect Peter Zumthor, and works as a consultant to the RIBA, advising on its awards programme.

SIR DAVID CHIPPERFIELD CBE, RA, RDI, RIBA is one of the UK's most lauded architects. He established David Chipperfield Architects in 1985; the practice has won more than 100 international awards and citations for design excellence, including the RIBA Stirling Prize in 2007 for the Museum of Modern Literature in Marbach am Neckar. Chipperfield has taught and lectured at schools of architecture worldwide. He was knighted in 2010 for services to architecture in the UK and Germany. In 2011 he received the Royal Gold Medal, given in recognition of a lifetime's work.

ACKNOWLEDGEMENTS AND PICTURE CREDITS

The author wishes to thank the four Awards Managers with whom he worked at the RIBA during the first twenty years of the Stirling Prize: Nancy Mills, Caz Facey, Clemency Christopherson and Jennifer Kean. Also, the three Event Managers: Juliette Runyeard, Sarah Davey and Marietjie Donaldson. Without their dedication and inspiration, none of this would have happened.

The RIBA wishes to thank all the awards judges, who give freely of their time and whose reports form the basis of much of the text of this book. The RIBA also thanks the photographers whose work is published in this book (credits appear in the individual entries or below), and who agreed to waive copyright fees for the reproduction of their work in connection with the RIBA's promotion of the awards.

The drawings and plans in this book have been reproduced courtesy of the architects for each project.

pp. 4–5: MAXXI, Museo Nazionale delle Arti del XXI Secolo, Rome, Italy, by Zaha Hadid Architects (see pp. 142–47); photo: Iwan Baan

pp. 8–9: Gateshead Millennium Bridge, Gateshead, Tyne and Wear, by Wilkinson Eyre Architects (see pp. 52–53); photo: Steve Mayes

pp. 12–13: Everyman Theatre, Hope Street, Liverpool, by Haworth Tompkins (see pp. 214–19); photo: Philip Vile

pp. 26–27: Ground-floor plan, American Air Museum in Britain, Imperial War Museum, Duxford, Cambridge, by Foster + Partners (see pp. 36–37)

pp. 68–69: New Area Terminal, Barajas Airport, Madrid, Spain, by Richard Rogers Partnership with Estudio Lamela (see pp. 70–75); photo: Manuel Renau

pp. 86–87: Museum of Modern Literature, Marbach am Necker, Germany, by David Chipperfield Architects (see pp. 88–93); photo: Christian Richters – VIEW

pp. 104–105: Nord Park Cable Railway, Innsbruck, Austria, by Zaha Hadid Architects (see pp. 116–17); photo: Hélène Binet

pp. 122–23: Liverpool One Masterplan, Liverpool 1, by BDP (masterplan architect; see pp. 138–39); photo: Grosvenor

pp. 140–41: MAXXI, Museo Nazionale delle Arti del XXI Secolo, Rome, Italy, by Zaha Hadid Architects (see pp. 142–47); photo: Roland Halbe

pp. 158–59: Roof cutaway, The Velodrome, Queen Elizabeth Olympic Park, London E20, by Hopkins Architects (see pp. 174–75)

pp. 176–77: Axonometric, Maggie's Glasgow, Gartnavel General Hospital, Great Western Road, Glasgow, by OMA (see pp. 188–89)

pp. 194–95: Newhall Be, Harlow, Essex, by Alison Brooks Architects (see pp. 206–207); photo: Paul Riddle – VIEW

pp. 212–13: Everyman Theatre, Hope Street, Liverpool, by Haworth Tompkins (see pp. 214–19); photo: Philip Vile

pp. 230–31: Darbishire Place, John Fisher Street, London E1, by Níall McLaughlin Architects (see pp. 238–39); photo: Níall McLaughlin

pp. 254–55: The Scottish Parliament, Horse Wynd, Edinburgh, by EMBT and RMJM (see pp. 64–65); photo: Keith Hunter

Photograph of David Chipperfield on p. 10: © Ingrid von Kruse. The images in the Introduction are copyright of the author, with the exception of the following pages: Clemency Christopherson: 25 top right; Paul Cochrane: 16, 23 centre right, 24 top, 25 bottom right; Simon Dewhurst: 23 bottom left; Andrew Hendry: 21 bottom right; 23 centre left, bottom right; Hodder + Partners: 15 bottom; RIBA: 15 top; Jonty Wilde: 23 top right.

Top image on p. 157 (Neues Museum, Berlin, Germany, by David Chipperfield Architects): © Candida Hoefer – VG Bild-Kunst, Bonn 2009. The image was originally commissioned for the book *Neues Museum Berlin*, edited by Rik Nys and Martin Reichert, published by Verlag der Buchhandlung Walther König in 2009.

First published 2016 by
Merrell Publishers,
London and New York

Merrell Publishers Limited
70 Cowcross Street
London EC1M 6EJ

merrellpublishers.com

in association with

RIBA
66 Portland Place
London W1B 1AD

architecture.com

British Library Cataloguing in
Publication Data. A catalogue
record for this book is available
from the British Library.

ISBN 978-1-8589-4654-2

Produced by Merrell Publishers Limited
Designed by Dennis and Nicola Bailey
Project-managed by Claire Chandler
Indexed by Vicki Robinson

Printed and bound in China